BIG
Book
of

HALLOWEEN

Better Homes and Gardens® Books
Des Moines, Iowa

BIG Book of HALLOWEEN

Better Homes and Gardens® Books
An imprint of Meredith® Books

Editor: Carol Field Dahlstrom
Writer: Susan M. Banker
Graphic Designer: Angela Haupert Hoogensen
Copy Chief: Terri Fredrickson
Copy and Production Editor: Victoria Forlini
Editorial Operations Manager: Karen Schirm
Managers, Book Production: Pam Kvitne,
    Marjorie J. Schenkelberg, Rick VonHoldt
Contributing Copy Editors: Arianna McKinney
Contributing Proofreaders: Karen Brewer
    Grossman, Colleen Johnson, Margaret Smith
Photographers: Andy Lyons Cameraworks, Peter
    Krumhardt, Scott Little
Technical Illustrator: Chris Neubauer Graphics, Inc.
Electronic Production Coordinator: Paula Forest
Editorial and Design Assistants: Kaye Chabot,
    Mary Lee Gavin, Karen McFadden

Meredith® Books
Publisher and Editor in Chief:
    Linda Raglan Cunningham
Design Director: Matt Strelecki
Executive Editor, Food and Crafts:
    Jennifer Dorland Darling

Publisher: James D. Blume
Executive Director, Marketing: Jeffrey Myers
Executive Director, New Business Development:
    Todd M. Davis
Executive Director, Sales: Ken Zagor
Director, Operations: George A. Susral
Director, Production: Douglas M. Johnston
Business Director: Jim Leonard

Vice President and General Manager:
    Douglas J. Guendel

Better Homes and Gardens® **Magazine**
Editor in Chief: Karol DeWulf Nickell

Meredith Publishing Group
President, Publishing Group: Stephen M. Lacy
Vice President-Publishing Director: Bob Mate

Meredith Corporation
Chairman and Chief Executive Officer:
    William T. Kerr

Chairman of the Executive Committee:
    E. T. Meredith III

All of us at Better Homes and Gardens® Books
are dedicated to providing you with information
and ideas to create beautiful and useful projects.
We welcome your comments and suggestions.
Write to us at: Better Homes and Gardens Books,
Crafts Editorial Department, 1716 Locust Street—
LN112, Des Moines, IA 50309-3023.

If you would like to purchase any of our crafts,
cooking, gardening, home improvement, or home
decorating and design books, check wherever
quality books are sold. Or visit us at:
bhgbooks.com

Our seal assures you that every
recipe in *Big Book of Halloween*
has been tested in the Better
Homes and Gardens® Test
Kitchen. This means that each
recipe is practical and reliable,
and meets our high standards of
taste appeal. We guarantee your satisfaction with
this book for as long as you own it.

make this Halloween
SPOOKTACULAR!

We all have our favorite Halloween tales—maybe it's that costume that made us feel like a princess or a scary game that made our spine tingle.

It's still so much fun to make the most of this frightfully fun holiday. Our kids can hardly wait to pick out pumpkins to take home and transform into something special. In this book we share dozens of ways to decorate these favorite symbols of the season—great carving and trimming ideas to really make them glow.

And if your family loves to gather in the kitchen to prepare Halloween foods, the recipes in this book are certain to become traditions. From snake bites bread to witch hat cake, you'll stir up a cauldron full of delicious foods with a Halloween flair.

You'll also discover "terrorific" party ideas, costumes to tempt everyone in the family, treat containers to surprise every boy and ghoul, and decorations for your own haunted mansion.

With hundreds of spirited ideas to choose from, your next Halloween is bound to be happy!

Enjoy the haunting season!

Carol Field Dahlstrom

contents

chapter 1

bootiful pumpkins

All dressed up and ready to glow

Paint them, trim them, carve them up right—you'll find loads of pumpkin ideas for Halloween night!

chapter 2

clever masks and costumes

Disguises for fun and fright

They're funny, silly, and some are really cool; these fantastic disguises won't make you a fool.

chapter 3

haunting decorations

Eeriesistible ideas to scare them silly

From funky wreaths to candles aglow—these Halloween trims will steal the show!

Pages 140–205

chapter 4

spooky treats and holders

Ghoulish goodies to concoct

Eerie breads, cookies, and dishes—oh, my! Give all of the recipes and holders a try.

Pages 206–257

chapter 5

terrorific parties and games

Fiendishly fun ideas to celebrate Halloween

From invitations to send away to fun games to play and play, your party will be a scream— a costume-wearer's dream!

Pages 258–285

bootiful

**all dressed up
and ready to glow**

pumpkins

Perched on a pumpkin house retreat, these lifelike artificial birds are ready for Halloween mischief. Great for a centerpiece or a last-minute trick-or-treat greeter, this quick pumpkin idea offers something to crow about.

supplies

Pumpkin
Knife, drill and large drill bit, or small, round cookie cutter
5-inch-long piece of ¼-inch dowel
Pencil sharpener
Paintbrush
Acrylic paints in black and white
3 artificial crows with wire feet
Scissors
Ruler
White paper
Tracing paper
Black marking pen
Medium-gauge wire
Round pencil
Nail
Raffia or straw

what to do

1 Cut a circle in the pumpkin on the lower half as shown, *opposite,* using a knife, a drill and bit, or a cookie cutter.

2 Sharpen one end of the dowel in a pencil sharpener. Paint the dowel black and let it dry. Add white dots by dipping the handle of a paintbrush into paint and dotting onto the dowel. Let dry. Insert the sharp end of the dowel just below the cutout. Attach a crow to the perch.

Firmly press the wire feet of the remaining crows into the pumpkin top.

3 To make a HAPPY HALLOWEEN sign, cut a 5×1⅝-inch piece from white paper. Trace the lettering, *below,* onto tracing paper. Place the traced pattern under white paper and hold up to a window for light. Use a black marking pen to copy the lettering. Outline the paper edges with marking pen. Poke two small holes in the top of the sign as shown, *opposite.* Cut an 8-inch length of wire. Curl it by wrapping around a pencil. Push the ends of the wire into the holes in the sign and twist to secure. Insert the nail into the pumpkin to hang the sign. Fill the hole with raffia or straw.

SIGN PATTERN

pumpkin pizzazz

Small pumpkins get big applause with simple-to-do techniques. The pumpkin, opposite, has Halloween words spelled out in alphabet macaroni and is highlighted with metallic paints.

The star version, below, becomes a dazzling delight covered with glistening stars of all colors.

spell-cast pumpkin

supplies
Pumpkin
Alphabet macaroni
Paintbrush
Glossy decoupage
  medium
Acrylic metallic paints
  in copper, green,
  purple, golden, or
  other desired colors
Pencil with round eraser

what to do
1 Decide what words or phrases to write on the pumpkin. Find the letters in the alphabet macaroni to spell out your selections. Use the paintbrush to stroke on a 1/8-inch-wide line of decoupage medium on the pumpkin where you want to place the macaroni. Place the macaroni letters on the decoupage medium, spelling out the Halloween words or phrases. Add selections until you like the look. Let the decoupage medium dry.

2 To color the macaroni letters, paint only the top surfaces, using very little metallic paint. Use only one color on the entire word or phrase so it stands out as a unit. Let the paint dry.

3 To make dots between the words, dip the pencil eraser into copper paint. Carefully dot the paint onto the surface of the pumpkin. Let the paint dry.

starstruck pumpkin

supplies
Star-shape gems
Silicone adhesive
Pumpkin

what to do
1 Turn all of the stars color side up. Decide how closely to place the stars.

2 Put a dab of silicone adhesive on the back of each star and press into place on the pumpkin. Let the glue dry.

spooky surprise

This friendly ghost, peeking from his pumpkin home, is fun to make from lightweight clay. With a few bright details, this ingenious pumpkin becomes the center of attention at your Halloween party.

supplies
Small pumpkin
Knife
Spoon
Four 8-inch-long pieces of ¼-inch dowel
Pencil sharpener
Acrylic paints in lime green and purple
Paintbrush
White air-dry clay, such as Crayola Model Magic clay
2 small black beads
1 large black bead
Toothpicks
Shredded colored paper

what to do

1 Cut the pumpkin in half horizontally, keeping the cut line as smooth as possible. Clean out the inside by scraping it with a spoon.

2 Sharpen both ends of the dowels in a pencil sharpener for easy insertion into the pumpkin. Paint two dowel pieces lime green and two purple. Let the paint dry. Dot each dowel by dipping the handle of the paintbrush into paint and dotting onto the dowel. Let the paint dry. Paint the pumpkin stem purple. Let dry. Paint green dots. Let dry. Insert the dowels into the bottom half of the pumpkin; then place the pumpkin top on by firmly pressing it onto the dowels.

3 To create the ghost, take a portion of clay suitable for the size of your pumpkin. Knead the clay until it is smooth. Shape the clay into a smooth oblong piece. Gently twist the top portion to create a ghostly head. Shape arms from small pieces of clay. Position the arms onto the ghost's body and press into place. Shape the bottom of the ghost to fit inside the pumpkin.

4 Use the photograph, *below,* as a guide to make the eyes and mouth. Press the black beads into the face using a toothpick. Press toothpicks into the bottom of the pumpkin. Position the ghost over the toothpicks and press into place.

5 Sprinkle shredded paper around pumpkin.

silver swirls

Long after the jack-o'-lantern candles are blown out, this silver-laden pumpkin will shine on. Use it as a beautiful centerpiece or autumn porch decoration perched on a bed of leaves or by itself. When the time comes to toss out the pumpkin, the solder swirls can be pulled out and saved to use year after year.

supplies

Lead-free solder in
  desired thicknesses
Wire cutters
Needlenose pliers
Ice pick
Pumpkin

what to do

1 Using the wire cutters, cut 2- to 8-inch lengths from the solder. Approximately 50 pieces are needed to trim a medium-size pumpkin like the one shown, *opposite.*

2 Using the photographs, *opposite* and *right,* as guides, twist the solder lengths into shapes using needlenose pliers to bend the end of the solder into a small loop. Bend the solder lengths into coils, S shapes, zigzags, or whatever you wish. Leave an inch at the end of the solder to bend perpendicular to the shape to poke into the pumpkin to hold the solder shape in place.

3 Use an ice pick to poke holes in the pumpkin, approximately 3 to 5 inches apart. Insert the bent ends of the solder shapes into the holes.

4 To attach a solder shape to the pumpkin stem, poke a hole in the stem using an ice pick. Shape a length of wire, leaving 1 inch at an end to insert into the stem. Push the solder into the stem.

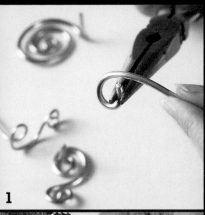

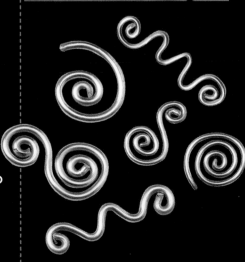

metal magic

Give a stylish twist to make any pumpkin stand out from the rest. Cut from copper foil, the leaves easily poke into a pumpkin top, opposite. The coordinating pair, left and below, takes only minutes using eyelets and grommets.

copper-leafed pumpkin

supplies

Tracing paper
Pencil
Old scissors
36-gauge copper tooling foil
Dish towel
Pointed skewer
20-gauge copper wire; ruler
Knife
Pumpkin

what to do

1 Trace the leaf patterns, *right,* onto tracing paper. Cut out shapes. Draw around leaf shapes on copper tooling foil. Cut out leaf shapes.

2 To make the leaf veins, place the leaves on a dish towel. Use the pattern to make vein impressions with a skewer.

3 Cut four 14-inch lengths of wire. Wrap the wire lengths around the skewer and remove. Pull apart as desired to make curlicues.

4 Cut two small slits, each about 1 inch long, next to the pumpkin stem. Insert one tip of each leaf into a slit. Shape leaves as desired.

5 Twist the ends of the wire curlicues together and press into the pumpkin near the leaves.

LEAF PATTERNS

rings pumpkins

supplies

Pumpkin
Gold grommets
Spoon, if needed
Gold and copper eyelets

what to do

1 Firmly push grommets into the pumpkin, spacing at least 1 inch apart. If the skin of the pumpkin is tough, use the back of a spoon to push the grommets through the skin.

2 Use eyelets to fill in around grommets. Or trim a miniature pumpkin using only eyelets.

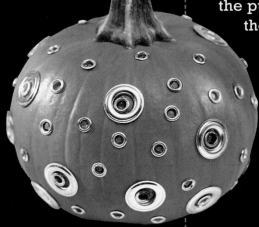

fallen leaves

The colors of autumn are vividly enhanced by painting gathered leaves with bright metallic paints. A white pumpkin creates an unexpected ghostlike backdrop for these favorite symbols of the fall season.

supplies

Dry leaves
Newspapers
Acrylic metallic paints
   in lime green,
   magenta, blue, and
   purple
Paintbrush
White pumpkin
Decoupage medium

what to do

1 Gather dry, but not brittle leaves in desired sizes and shapes. Green leaves may curl and will not accept paint well.

2 Cover your work surface with newspapers. Paint the front sides of the leaves using metallic paints. Let the paint dry. Apply a second coat if needed. Let the paint dry. Turn the leaves over and paint the backs, using the same color. Let the paint dry.

3 Paint the stem of the pumpkin using the desired color of metallic paint. Let the paint dry.

4 To attach the leaves to the top and sides of the pumpkin, coat the back of each leaf with decoupage medium. The leaves will curl a bit rather than stay flat to the pumpkin. Press leaves onto the pumpkin and paint over the front of the leaves with a coat of decoupage medium. Let the decoupage medium dry.

patterned pair

Brushstrokes of metallic paint lends a contemporary flair to this beauty from the pumpkin patch. The details complementing the checkerboard pattern are easy-to-do dots and scribbles made using a permanent marking pen.

Colorful plastic-coated wires seem to grow on the miniature pumpkin. Holes poked in the pumpkin anchor the vertical wires, and more wires twist around the stem.

check-it-out pumpkin

supplies
Acrylic metallic paints
  in teal and purple
1-inch flat paintbrush
Pumpkin
Metallic gold
  permanent marking
  pen
Pencil with
  round eraser

what to do
1 Paint a teal checkerboard design on the pumpkin. Starting at the center of the pumpkin, paint 1-inch squares around the center. Continue making 1-inch squares around the pumpkin as shown, *opposite.* Let the paint dry.

2 To make scribbles, draw them on the painted squares. Let them dry.

3 To add dots between the painted squares, dip the eraser end of a pencil into purple paint. Carefully dot on the surface. Let the paint dry.

wire-wrapped pumpkin

supplies
Ice pick
Miniature pumpkin
Plastic-coated wires in
  teal and purple
Scissors

what to do
1 Using an ice pick, poke tiny holes at the top of each pumpkin groove around the stem and along the bottom of the pumpkin.

2 Cut lengths of wire 2 inches longer than distance from top hole to bottom hole. Bend over 1 inch at the end of a wire length. Push the bent end into a hole at the top of the pumpkin. Gently pull the wire down the groove of the pumpkin and firmly push the remaining wire end into the hole at the bottom for each set of holes.

3 Cut a 3-inch piece of each color of wire. Twist together at one end. Wrap around stem.

kooky characters

This pair of pumpkins makes quite a team when sitting piggyback. Their playful expressions make them appear as if they're sharing the latest Halloween gags. Our Golden Girl, right, is all dressed up with curly locks and a pretty bow.

joking, jesting buddies

supplies

Knife
Large round pumpkin
Large tall pumpkin
Spoon
Fine permanent marking pen
2 votive candles
Matches

what to do

1 Cut the top off each pumpkin and scoop out the insides using a spoon. Place the tall pumpkin on top of the round pumpkin. If necessary, enlarge the hole in the top of the round pumpkin so the tall one sits as shown, *opposite.*

2 Looking at the photograph, *opposite,* draw faces on the pumpkins so that they look as if they're talking to each other. Cut out face shapes using a knife.

3 Place a candle in the round jack-o'-lantern and light. Position the tall pumpkin on it. Place a candle in the tall jack-o'-lantern and light it. Put on the lid. Never leave a burning candle unattended.

golden girl

supplies

Small round pumpkin
Black eyelets
Black pipe cleaners
Round pencil, dowel, or skewer
Ice pick
Scissors
12-inch pieces of ribbon

what to do

1 Push an eyelet into the center of the pumpkin for the nose. Using the photograph, *above,* as a guide, make two triangular eyes and a smile using eyelets.

2 To make the hair, tightly wrap each pipe cleaner around a pencil, dowel, or skewer. Use an ice pick to make holes in the top of the pumpkin for hair. Push the ends of the pipe cleaners into the holes. For bangs, cut pipe cleaners in half.

3 Tie two or three ribbons to the stem to trail through the hair.

web-laden pumpkin

Glitter paint and faceted gems sparkle with vibrant color on this spider and web pumpkin. The web effect is easy to achieve by outlining the pumpkin seams with a paint pen.

supplies
Pumpkin
Metallic paint pens in purple and gold
Gems in oval and rectangular shapes
Small metallic beads to match gems

what to do

1 To draw the spiderweb, use metallic purple paint pen, following the vertical seams in the pumpkin. Use the photographs, *opposite* and *right,* as guides, making the lines different lengths. When all of the vertical lines are painted, draw the horizontal lines, making them slightly scalloped and about 1 inch apart. Let the paint dry.

2 Decide where to position spiders. Place a small amount of metallic gold paint pen on the back of the gem for body. Use an oval gem for a large spider or a rectangular gem for a small spider. Place on the pumpkin. If making a large spider, use a rectangular gem for the head. Place paint pen on the back of the gem and position gem above the oval body. Outline the spiders using metallic gold paint pen. Press two bead eyes to the top of the head. Draw paint pen legs and let dry.

3 Paint the stem of the pumpkin using metallic gold paint pen. Let the paint dry.

glowing stars

Master the trick to this pumpkin by using cookie cutters to make the star shapes. The larger stars are carved through the entire pumpkin skin and flesh, while the smaller ones leave a thin layer of pumpkin flesh for the light to glow through.

supplies
Knife; pumpkin
Spoon
Star cookie cutters
Paring knife
Tracing paper; pencil
Scissors; metallic gold
  permanent marking
  pen; toothpick
Candle; match

what to do
1 Cut the top third off the pumpkin. Clean out the insides using a spoon.

2 Press a large cookie cutter into the pumpkin. Remove the cookie cutter and use a paring knife to carefully cut out the shapes. If you do not have star cookie cutters, trace the patterns, *right.* Cut out patterns and trace star shapes on the pumpkin using gold marking pen. Use a knife to cut shapes from pumpkin.

3 For the small stars, press the small star cookie cutter into the skin of the pumpkin, being careful not to pierce through the entire skin. Use a paring knife to remove the outer layer of skin, leaving a thin lining for light to shine through.

4 Outline the star shapes with a gold marking pen. Use the marker to make squiggles between the star shapes, if desired.

5 Poke a toothpick into the bottom of one of the stars removed from the pumpkin. Color in the star shape using metallic gold marking pen. Color the raised areas of the stem.

6 Use a toothpick to poke a hole in the top of the stem. Insert the toothpick with the star on the end.

7 Place a candle inside the pumpkin, light the wick, and place the lid on the pumpkin. Never leave a burning candle unattended.

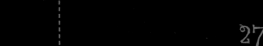

STAR PATTERNS

jack-o'-jester

Any pumpkin, carved or fresh from the pumpkin patch, looks grand sitting upon this festive garden post. Trimmed with wood stars and beads on colored wires, the brightly painted post stands 4 feet tall.

supplies
Pumpkin
Knife
Spoon
Wood garden post
Saw; sandpaper
11-inch square of ¾-inch pine
Flower-shape wood clock face or 9-inch square of ¾-inch pine
Band saw; tack cloth
Acrylic paints in orange, black, yellow, purple, green, and white
Paintbrush
Pencil; scissors
Tracing paper, if needed
Four 3-inch wood stars
Five 1¾-inch wood stars
Twenty ¾-inch wood stars
Wood finial
Wood glue
Drill and drill bit

Two 2-inch-long wood screws with flat heads
Screwdriver
Assorted beads
Colored wire
Ice pick
Toothpick
Candle
Match

what to do

1 Cut the top off the pumpkin in a zigzag pattern. Clean out the insides with a spoon. Carve a face on the pumpkin. Set it aside.

2 If desired, cut off the bottom of the garden post so it measures approximately 4 feet high. Sand any rough spots on the garden post, clock face, or remaining pine pieces. Remove dust using a tack cloth.

3 Using the photograph, *right,* for ideas, paint the garden post. Paint solid areas, checks, stripes, dots, or whatever you wish. To make the triangular shapes at the top of the large stars, paint them green with a little yellow mixed in. Let the paint dry. Outline the lower edges of the

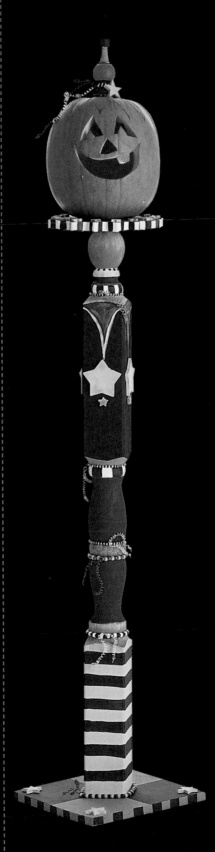

continued on page 31

STAND TOP PATTERN

FOLD

triangles with yellow. For all other green painted areas, highlight with yellow while the green paint is wet. For the yellow areas, add dabs of orange while the yellow paint is wet. When painting a black-and-white check pattern, paint the entire area white first. When dry, fill in the black checks.

4 For the base, draw pencil lines to divide the base into four equal sections. Paint two opposite corners orange and the remaining two black. Let the paint dry. Paint the edges with black and orange, creating a check pattern. Let the paint dry.

5 For the wood piece that sits on the top of the post, use the wood clock face. If you prefer to cut a top piece from pine, trace the pattern, *opposite.* Cut out the pattern and trace around it on pine. Use a band saw to cut out the shape. Sand the edges if necessary. Paint the top solid purple and the edge a black-and-white check design. Let the paint dry.

Paint orange and green dots to the top edge if desired. Let dry.

6 Paint the large and medium stars yellow. Dry-brush the edges orange. Let the paint dry. Paint 12 of the small stars orange and the remaining stars yellow. Paint yellow on the edges of the orange stars and orange on the edges of the yellow stars. Let dry.

7 Paint the finial as desired, using the photograph, *page 28,* for ideas. Let the paint dry.

8 Glue the large stars on the garden post below the green triangles. Add a small star below each large one. Glue a medium star in each corner of the base piece. Glue small stars around the edge of the top piece, alternating orange and yellow stars. Let dry.

9 Drill a hole through the center of the top piece. Drill a hole in the center of the top and bottom of the post. Drill a hole through the center of the base piece. Use screws to secure the top and base to the post. Tighten to secure.

10 Thread enough beads on wire to wrap around post where desired. Tie the wires in place. To curl the wire ends, wrap tightly around an ice pick.

11 Use an ice pick to poke a hole 1 inch deep in the stem of the pumpkin. Glue a toothpick in the hole. Place painted finial on toothpick. Add beaded wires and a wooden star to the finial.

12 Carefully place the pumpkin on stand, making sure it is balanced. Set a candle in the pumpkin and light it. Put on the lid. Never leave a burning candle unattended.

party pumpkins

Whether resting on the front stoop or on your party table, these pumpkins delight one and all. Within minutes make either of these unusual pumpkins.

color-blast pumpkin

supplies
Pumpkin
Quilting pins with
  colored heads
Craft foam shapes
Gold flathead
  straight pins

what to do
1 Secure foam shapes to the pumpkin with a quilting pin through each center.
2 Between foam shapes, poke three gold pins into pumpkin in a triangular shape.

paint-drip pumpkin

supplies
Newspapers
Pumpkin
Gold spray paint
Lime green glass spray
  paint
White acrylic paint
Paintbrush
White glitter paint

what to do
1 In a well-ventilated work area, cover work surface with newspapers. Lightly spray the top portion of the pumpkin with gold spray paint. Let dry.
2 Lightly spray a lime green glass paint over the gold area. Let dry.
3 Paint small drips and dots with white acrylic paint. Let dry. Paint over white acrylic paint with white glitter paint. Let dry.

joyful pumpkins

The stacked-up pumpkin pals, opposite, make you giggle right along with them, while glittery purple polka dots add razzle-dazzle to the striking pumpkin, below.

stacked-up pumpkins

supplies

Large, medium, and
 small pumpkins
Carving knife
Spoon
Candles
Beaded garland
Long-handled matches

what to do

1 Cut the top off each pumpkin and scoop out the insides. Stack the pumpkins by size. Trim the top holes, if necessary, so they sit firmly together. Dismantle the trio.

2 Carve faces in the pumpkins. Place a candle in each pumpkin. Carefully restack the pumpkins.

3 Wrap the pumpkin trio with a long beaded garland as shown, *opposite*.

4 Light the candles through the openings. Place the lid on the top pumpkin. Never leave burning candles unattended.

polka-dot pumpkin

supplies

Newspapers
Pumpkin
Gold spray paint
Purple glitter
 paint
Paintbrush

what to do

1 In a well-ventilated work area, cover work surface with newspapers. Lightly spray the top portion of the pumpkin with gold spray paint. Let dry.

2 Paint on polka dots with purple glitter paint. Let dry.

hydrangea pumpkin

A cloud of hydrangeas makes a beautiful presentation for the autumn table when tucked into the top of a natural green and orange pumpkin.

supplies
Medium or large green and orange pumpkin
Sharp knife
Spoon
Scissors
Fresh-cut or artificial hydrangea
Plastic liner, optional

what to do

1 Cut a circle around the pumpkin stem. Scoop out the pumpkin using a spoon.

2 Use scissors to cut the hydrangea stems to an appropriate length when placed inside the pumpkin. If using fresh-cut flowers, place a plastic liner in the pumpkin before arranging the flowers.

grommet and eyelet gourds

supplies

Gourds
Gold grommets
Eyelets in gold, silver, black, copper, and white
Embroidery floss in orange and purple
Black craft wire
Wire cutters

what to do

1 For the tall gourd, press five grommets equally spaced around the center of the gourd. Press five more grommets 1 inch above the first row, centering them between the grommets in the first row. Wind orange floss around the grommets as shown, *above*.

2 For the green gourd, press 10 gold eyelets equally spaced around the center of the gourd. Press 10 more eyelets ¾ inch above the first row, centering them between the eyelets in the first row. Wind purple floss around the eyelets.

3 For the orange gourd, randomly press silver, white, copper, and black eyelets into the gourd. Cut a 10-inch piece of wire. Wrap the center of the wire around the stem. Coil the ends.

swirl-top pumpkin

Both classy and easy, this glistening pumpkin will delight all autumn long. Metallic red spray paint highlights the pumpkin top, acting as a backdrop for golden swirls of glitter paint to dance around the stem.

supplies
Pumpkin
Newspapers
Metallic red spray paint
Gold glitter fabric
 paint pen

what to do

1 Wash the pumpkin to remove any surface dirt. Let the pumpkin dry.

2 In a well-ventilated work area, cover the work surface with newspapers. Place the pumpkin in the center of the newspapers.

3 Lightly spray the top of the pumpkin with metallic red spray paint. Let the paint dry.

4 Use a gold glitter paint pen to draw swirls or other designs over the painted area of the pumpkin. Define the stem with paint pen details. Let the paint dry.

elegant pumpkins

For a fanciful presentation, dress up bright orange pumpkins in glistening metallic beads, gold foil leafing, stars, and ribbon. They set a festive mood all autumn long.

beaded pumpkins

supplies
Large and small pumpkins
Beaded garland
Straight pins
Wide wire-edge ribbon
Star sequins
Quilting pins
Beading wire; beads

what to do
1 For the large pumpkin, pin one end of the garland at the stem base. Loop the garland down halfway, bring back up to the stem, and pin. Continue making loops around the pumpkin top. Tie a generous ribbon bow around the stem.

2 For the small pumpkin, attach star sequins with quilting pins. Thread beads on three lengths of wire. Add a star sequin and bead to one end of each wire. Thread wire back through star and beads to secure. Poke other end of wire into pumpkin next to the stem. Secure a bead and star on the end of a piece of wire. Poke into stem and shape as desired.

gilded pumpkins

supplies
Dry, firm pumpkins
Adhesive for gold leafing
Paintbrush
Gold foil leafing

what to do
1 Paint the pumpkin top with a coat of adhesive for gold leafing. When tacky, turn over the pumpkin and paint the bottom. Let the adhesive dry to a tacky stage.

2 Gently apply gold foil leafing in small pieces to the tacky surface, smoothing out the wrinkles until the pumpkin is completely covered.

painted pumpkins

These miniature works of art incorporate your favorite motifs and colors. Decorate them with paint to leave creative hints of autumn all around the house.

supplies

Dry, firm small pumpkins

Acrylic paints in black, white, red, green, purple, aqua, or other colors
Pencil
Paintbrushes

what to do

1 Decide what to paint on the pumpkin, using star, zigzag, diamond, stripe, or dotted designs.

2 Paint the background areas and let dry. To make dots, dip the eraser of a pencil or the handle of a paintbrush into paint and dot onto the surface. Make double dots by painting smaller dots over larger ones, letting dry between coats. Use a fine liner brush to make stripes and outlines. Let the paint dry.

wacky wired gourds

Available in a rainbow of metallic colors, shiny craft wire electrifies this pair of gourds.

supplies
Wire cutters
Ruler
Fine-weight colored
  metallic wire
  (available at crafts and
  art stores)
Ice pick
Miniature pumpkins

what to do

1 For the striped coil pumpkin, cut 8-inch lengths of wire. Wrap each length tightly around the ice pick, leaving 1 inch straight on each end. Make six to nine coils. To place on pumpkin, use the ice pick to poke holes around the stem and at the bottom of the pumpkin, following the seams of the pumpkin. Poke a wire end in each hole to secure.

2 For the swirl pumpkin, cut a 14-inch length of wire. Fold the wire in half. Form each end into a swirl. Shape small loops between the swirls. Use an ice pick to poke a hole in the top of the pumpkin near the stem. Push the center fold of the wire into the hole.

peekaboo pumpkin

Fun for a Halloween party or any autumn get-together, these silly characters are right at home in their stout pumpkin birdhouse.

supplies
Pumpkin
Knife or drill with 1¼-inch bit
Spoon
Acrylic paints in black, lavender, blue, green, pink, yellow, or other colors
Paintbrush
Five 1¼-inch wood doll heads
Thick white crafts glue
¼-inch plastic wiggly eyes
Air-dry clay, such as Crayola Model Magic
Scissors
Thick lead-free solder wire or armature wire
Ruler
Wire cutters
Large marking pen or 1-inch dowel
Pencil, if needed

what to do

1 Cut a small hole in the bottom of the pumpkin. Remove the bottom piece of pumpkin shell. Clean out the inside of the pumpkin using a spoon. Cut or drill five 1¼-inch holes randomly around the pumpkin.

2 To make the bird heads, paint each wood doll head with the desired color. Let dry. Glue on two wiggly eyes as shown, *opposite* and *below.*

3 Shape beaks from small pieces of clay about the size of a grape. Shape the clay into cones and slice narrow ends with scissors, beginning at the tips. Avoid slicing all the way across. Spread the clay apart to form open beaks. Let the clay dry. Paint the beaks yellow or black. Let the paint dry. Glue the beaks onto the bird heads below the eyes. Let the glue dry.

4 Cut five wire pieces 4 to 8 inches long. To form into a coil, wrap each around a large marking pen or 1-inch dowel. Insert one end of the wire into the hole in the back of the wood bird head, widening the hole with a pencil if needed. Glue the wire in place. Insert the other end of the wire into the pumpkin inside each hole.

pumpkin topiary

Welcome autumn and Halloween visitors with an arrangement that takes advantage of the season's harvest. Miniature gourds are readily available at farmer's markets and grocery stores in the fall.

supplies

Wire clothes hanger
Wire cutters; ruler
3 miniature pumpkins in graduated sizes
Hot-glue gun and glue sticks
Green acrylic paint
Sea sponge or cellulose sponge
Small terra-cotta pot
Crafts foam
U-pins
Silk or fresh autumn leaves
Raffia
Bittersweet

what to do

1 Cut two 2-inch pieces of wire from a clothes hanger as shown in Photo 1, *right.*

2 Insert one end of a piece of wire into or beside the stem of the bottom pumpkin. Place a drop of glue where the wire enters the pumpkin as shown in Photo 2.

3 Insert the other end of the wire into the bottom of the middle pumpkin (Photo 3).

4 Attach the top pumpkin to the middle pumpkin in the same manner.

5 Using the sea sponge, pat green paint onto the terra-cotta pot, allowing the clay color to show through. If desired, use a cellulose sponge by tearing away pieces from the surface to roughen it.

6 Fill the pot almost to the top with crafts foam. Pin a collar of leaves to the foam with U-pins. Insert a short piece of clothes hanger wire into the bottom pumpkin. Push the other end into the crafts foam. Tie raffia around the rim of the pot and glue sprigs of bittersweet to the raffia.

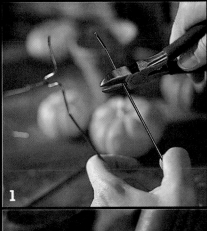

1

2

3

funky punkin stand

Enjoy pulling out this striking stand from your bag of tricks each Halloween. Then decorate a pumpkin to set on top for a spirited duo.

supplies

Two 9½-inch wood plates
Pencil
Ruler
**Drill; ⅛- and
  1/16-inch drill bits**
7-inch stool leg
Two 1-inch wood screws
Screwdriver
Wood glue
Black spray paint
Decoupage medium
Paintbrush
**Glitter in purple, orange,
  lime green, and black**
Silver glitter glue
**16 gems (8 gold and
  8 purple)**
Copper wire; wire cutters
Needlenose pliers
Metallic purple beads
Pumpkin

what to do

1 To make the stand, mark the center of each wood plate. Using a ⅛-inch bit, drill a hole in the center of each plate. Using wood screws, attach the plates to the stool leg, plate bottoms facing the leg ends. Dab wood glue to the ends of the stool leg before tightening the screws. Let dry.

2 In a well-ventilated work area, spray-paint the stand black. Let dry.

3 On the stand top, measure and mark 16 equally spaced dots ¼ inch in from the edge. Using a 1/16-inch bit, drill a hole at each dot.

4 On the rim of the top plate, brush on decoupage medium. While wet, sprinkle with purple glitter. Shake different colors of glitter on the stool leg, working on one section at a time. To make stripes on the base plate, paint wide stripes approximately 1 inch apart using decoupage medium. Sprinkle with purple glitter. Make narrow green glitter stripes between the purple stripes. Let dry.

5 Between each drilled hole, dab a pea-size dot of glitter glue. Place a gem on each dot of glue, alternating gold and purple. Let dry.

6 Cut sixteen 6-inch-long pieces of wire. Using needlenose pliers, coil one end of each wire, leaving 1 inch straight. Slip a bead on the straight end. Poke each wire up through a hole in the top plate. Use the pliers to make a small loop at the ends of wires to secure.

7 To trim the pumpkin, use a pencil to draw a checkerboard on the pumpkin. Using decoupage medium, paint two or three squares and then sprinkle with black glitter. Continue until the design is complete. Create purple glitter triangles, squares, and rectangles in between the black areas. Paint decoupage medium on the stem and sprinkle with green glitter. Let dry.

glowing pumpkins

Glowing candles are a must at Halloween, and a glowing candelabra or pumpkin trio is just right for the eerie occasion.

pumpkin candelabra

supplies

Small pumpkins, one for
  each candelabra holder
Knife
Drill and large bit
Pony beads; sequins
Quilting pins
Iron candelabra
Short taper candles
Ribbon; matches

what to do

1 Wash and dry the pumpkins. Cut off the stems. Drill holes large enough to hold a candle in each pumpkin top.

2 Use pins to attach beads and sequins randomly to the pumpkins.

3 Place pumpkins on candelabra holders. Insert a candle in each top. Tie a ribbon bow around the center of the candelabra. Light the candles. Never leave burning candles unattended.

jesting jack-o'-lanterns

supplies
3 pumpkins
  approximately the
  same size
Carving knife
Spoon
Candles
Matches

what to do

1 Decide how you want the trio arranged. Trim off one side of each outer pumpkin so they can sit close together. Cut the bottom off the center pumpkin.

2 Scoop out the insides of the pumpkins. Carve faces on the pumpkins.

3 Place candles in each of the pumpkins. Light the candles. Never leave burning candles unattended.

sequin stripe

As elegant as a dancer's dress, this pumpkin wears stripes of sequins in silver and black.

supplies
Tape measure
Pumpkin
Strung sequins in silver and black
Scissors
Straight pins with black heads
Silver cord

what to do
1 Measure the pumpkin from the stem to the bottom center. Use this measurement to cut lengths from the sequin strings.

2 Using the pumpkin seams as guides, pin the sequins vertically on the pumpkin, alternating colors.

3 Wrap the stem with silver cord. Use pins to secure the ends.

autumn-hue gourds

Produce masterpieces on gourd canvases without being a professional artist!

supplies
Small dried ornamental gourds
Plastic scraper
Sharp knife; pencil
Assorted leaves
Wood-burning tool with fine tip
Watercolor marking pens in purple, pink, red, green, orange, and yellow
Medium-size soft paintbrush
Clear varnish

what to do
1 Choose gourds with a fairly smooth, clean surface. They should be dry, hard, and hollow-sounding. Soak and clean the gourds with warm, soapy water using a plastic scraper. Scrape off any rough areas with a sharp knife. Wipe dry.

2 Using a pencil, trace around the leaves on the gourds.

3 Using a wood-burning tool with a fine tip, outline the leaf shapes and draw in veins. Using the photo, *above,* for inspiration, color the outlined areas with watercolor marking pens, overlapping colors slightly. To create a shaded look, color purple next to pink or red and green next to orange or yellow.

4 Dip a medium-size soft paintbrush in water and wipe off the excess. Brush onto the areas covered with marking pens to blend colors. Let dry.

5 Brush a coat of clear varnish over the gourds, blending the colors once again. Do not overbrush or the colors will become muddy and run.

53

starstruck pumpkins

Carved, painted, or wrapped in sequins, these star-embellished pumpkins are stunning alone or in a grouping.

supplies

Pumpkins of all sizes
Fabric paint pen in
 desired color
Paring knife
Spoon
Votive candle; matches
Star sequins
Pearl-head quilting pins
Small star cookie cutter

what to do

1 To make the paint-pen pumpkin, draw stars in desired colors all over the pumpkin. Let the paint dry.

2 To make the candleholder pumpkin, use a paring knife to cut a round hole large enough to hold a votive candle. Use a spoon to scoop out enough space to insert candle. Decorate around the hole with paint pen as desired. Place a votive candle into the hole.

3 To make the sequined pumpkin, attach star sequins using quilting pins.

4 To make the cookie-cutter pumpkin, press the star cookie cutter into the surface of the pumpkin and remove the skin of the star shape using a paring knife. Repeat as desired. Never leave burning candles unattended.

gourd ghouls

PUMPKIN

ARM FOR TALL GOURD

HAT BRIM

ARM FOR SHORT GOURD

BAT

These playful pranksters will cause you to cackle with delight. Made from small gourds, the fiendish duo is trimmed with craft foam accents.

supplies

Small pear-shape gourds
White spray primer
Paper punch
Craft foam in white, black, orange, and yellow; scissors
White map pins
Fine-line black permanent marking pen
Tracing paper; pencil
Thick white crafts glue
Acrylic paints in black and white; paintbrush
Colored wire in orange and purple
Clothespin

what to do

1 In a well-ventilated work area, spray-paint the gourds white. Let dry.

2 To make eyes, punch out black circles from crafting foam. Using the photo, *opposite,* for placement, attach the black circles to the gourds using white map pins. Use a black marking pen to draw mouths and make a dot for each nose.

3 Trace the patterns, *right.* Cut out. Trace around the patterns on craft foam. Cut out the shapes. Glue the details on the pumpkin shape. Let dry. To make eyes on the bat, dip the handle of a paintbrush into white paint and dot onto the foam. When dry, make a tiny black dot in the center of each eye using a black marking pen.

4 To coil wire, wrap the entire orange wire around a pencil and remove. For the purple wire, wrap half of the wire. Shape the remaining end into a zigzag, making a spiral at the end. Glue the jack-o'-lantern to the end of the purple coil. Glue the bat to one end of the orange coil. Let dry.

5 Pin the arms into place. For the tall gourd, place the orange wire coil into position. Glue the right foam hand over the wire, securing with a clothespin until dry.

6 Slip hat brim over the top of the short gourd. Paint the gourd black above the brim. Let dry. Slip the purple wire into place.

7 If the gourds roll, poke pins into the bottoms to steady them.

sparkling pumpkins

Pumpkins of any size become glamorous instantly with glittery stems draped with curling ribbon.

supplies
Pumpkin with long stem
Paintbrush
White glue
Glitter in purple, lime green, or other color
Silver curling ribbon
Scissors

what to do
1 Choose a pumpkin with a long stem. Wash and dry the pumpkin.

2 Use a paintbrush to apply glue to the stem. While the glue is wet, sprinkle with glitter. Let dry.

3 Cut 2-foot lengths of ribbon. To curl pieces of ribbon, hold scissors at an angle against ribbon, pulling ribbon taut against blade. Place one or two ribbons around the stem.

darling in daisies

Abloom with autumn flowers, this no-carve pumpkin can be put together at the last minute.

supplies
Pumpkin
Knife; spoon
Drill and ¼-inch bit
Scissors; daisies

what to do

1 Cut the top off the pumpkin. Scoop out the seeds and pulp. Using a drill, make holes randomly around the pumpkin.

2 Cut stems of daisies to appropriate length for the pumpkin. Push stems through the holes, arranging as desired.

charmed box

When the light falls upon this paper pumpkin, the glitter will sparkle with vibrant color. Use it to hold Halloween treasures or candy for your favorite kids in costume.

supplies

Hollow brown paper pumpkin (available in crafts stores)
Pencil
Ruler
Sharp utility or crafts knife
Acrylic paints in orange, green, and white
Paintbrush
Awl
White glue
Glitter in orange and green
Wire
Wire cutters
Pliers

what to do

1 Draw a horizontal line around the paper pumpkin to indicate where to cut it in half. Cut along the line with a sharp utility or crafts knife.

2 Paint the outside of the pumpkin orange. Paint the inside green. Make white highlights if desired. Let the paint dry.

3 Use an awl to pierce holes through the stem and on each side of the bottom piece as shown, *opposite,* to insert wire.

4 Coat the outside of the pumpkin and stem with white glue. Sprinkle orange and green glitters onto the wet glue. Let the glue dry.

5 Cut a piece of wire approximately 20 inches long. Insert the wire into the hole in the pumpkin stem. Wrap the wire ends around a pencil three or four times to make a coil. Insert the wire ends into the holes in the bottom piece. To secure, pinch the ends up with pliers. Adjust the lid as desired.

jeweled pumpkin

For an opulent pumpkin that shimmers with color, display glass beads in diamond-shape windows trimmed with upholstery tacks.

supplies
Pumpkin
Sharp knife
Spoon or ice cream scoop
Tracing paper
Pencil
Scissors
Crafting wire
Wire cutters
Ruler
Assorted translucent colored glass beads
1½-inch eye pins
Upholstery tacks
Candle
Matches

what to do

1 Cut off the bottom of the pumpkin. Scoop out the seeds and pulp.

2 Trace the diamond pattern, *right.* Cut out.

3 Trace the diamond pattern vertically onto the pumpkin three or four times. Cut out the shapes using a knife.

4 For each center beaded row, cut a 5½-inch piece of wire. Thread beads on wire leaving approximately 1 inch free on each end. Poke one end of the beaded wire into the lower point of the diamond. Bend the wire slightly to enable the top of the wire to be inserted into the top of the diamond as shown in Photo 1, *right.*

5 For each short beaded row, thread beads on an eye pin. As shown in Photo 2, poke the straight end of the pin into the top of the diamond, one on each side of the center row.

6 Push an upholstery tack into the pumpkin at each point of the diamond. Push an upholstery tack midway at each point. Place a candle in the pumpkin and light it. Never leave burning candles unattended.

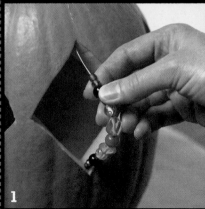

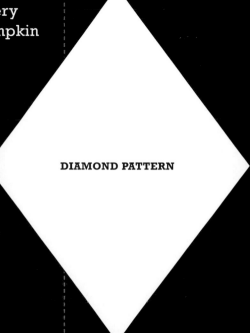

DIAMOND PATTERN

little critter lodge

Create a vivacious
pumpkin full of
personality with these
nutty little characters.

supplies
Tall pumpkin
Marking pen
Knife
Spoon
Thick pink craft foam
Scissors
Thick white crafts glue
Acorns, pecans, English
   walnut, almonds,
   chestnuts, pistachios,
   and allspice
Glossy acrylic paints in
   desired colors
Paintbrush
Pipe cleaners
Toothpicks
Candle
Matches

what to do

1 Using the photo, *opposite,* for ideas, draw a door and windows on the pumpkin. Cut out a circular shape from the bottom of pumpkin. Scoop out the insides. Cut out the shapes.

2 From craft foam, cut rectangular shutters with one rounded corner. Draw shutter lines with a marking pen. Glue shutters by the window openings.

3 To make critters, glue nuts together. For the critter at the door, use half a walnut shell with an almond for the body and an acorn for the head. For critters with ears, use pistachio shells for the ears. Use allspice for eyes and noses. Draw details with marking pen. When glue is dry, paint as desired. Paint stem green. Let dry. For the door critter, glue on pipe cleaner arms and legs. Use toothpicks to support the critters if needed. Never leave burning candles unattended.

the pumpkin king

Crown this no-carve king with a collar that's normally used in ductwork.

supplies
Tracing paper
Pencil
Pumpkin
Permanent marking
  pens in black, blue,
  and white

6-inch start collar with crimp (found with the aluminum ductwork supplies in hardware and home center stores)
Strong adhesive, such as E6000
Gems in assorted sizes, shapes, and colors

what to do

1 Enlarge and trace the pattern, *below.* Place the pattern on the pumpkin, pencil side down. Trace over the lines to transfer the pattern.

2 Outline the pattern lines with black marking pen. Color in the eyes using blue. Color in the whites of the eyes. Let the marking pen lines dry.

3 Glue gems around the start collar as desired. Let the glue dry. Place the crown on the pumpkin.

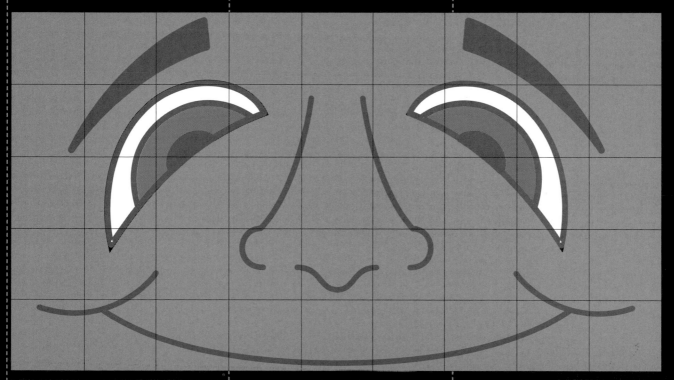

THE PUMPKIN KING FACE PATTERN

1 SQUARE = 1 INCH

finial stems

Use these striking pumpkin stems year after year. Just unscrew the stems and save them for the next haunting season.

supplies
Utility knife
Pumpkins
Scrap piece of board
Drill and 1/8-inch
  drill bit
Wood finials
Newspapers
White spray primer
Acrylic paints in black,
  white, orange, purple,
  green, and yellow
Paintbrushes
Glossy acrylic sealer

what to do

1 Using a utility knife, cut the stem off each pumpkin, cutting as close to the pumpkin as possible.

2 To keep finials upright while painting, drill holes in a scrap piece of board, leaving at least 6 inches between holes. Screw the finials into the board until secure.

3 In a well-ventilated work area, cover the work surface with newspapers. Spray a coat of primer on the finials. Let the paint dry.

4 Paint each finial black or white. Let dry.

5 Using the photograph, *opposite,* for ideas, paint various colored checks, dots, swirls, or other desired motifs on the finials. Let the paint dry.

6 Paint a coat of acrylic sealer on each finial. Let the sealer dry. Paint on a second coat and let dry.

7 Screw a finial into the top of the pumpkin where the stem was removed.

haunted pumpkin

Fit for ghouls of every sort, this miniature mansion makes a most haunting centerpiece.

supplies

Tracing paper
Pencil
Scissors
Heavy black paper
Ruler
$\frac{1}{8}$-inch square dowel
Saw
Thick white crafts glue
Acrylic paints in purple, green, orange, and white
Paintbrush
Alphabet macaroni
4-inch-long metal banner and a 1$\frac{1}{2}$-inch-wide metal sign (available with the miniatures in crafts stores)
Medium-size pumpkin
Brush-on white glitter
8-inch foam wreath
Assorted dried flowers
Miniature tree (available in crafts shops with the miniature village items)

what to do

1 Trace the patterns, *right.* Cut out. Trace the shapes on black paper and cut out. Cut an 8$\frac{1}{2}$×5$\frac{1}{2}$-inch piece of black paper for roof.

2 Cut pieces of dowel for frames and crossbars for windows and door. Glue in place. Let dry.

3 Paint the dowel pieces purple. Let dry. Add green stripes. Let dry. Paint orange checks along the edge of the roof. Let dry.

4 Glue alphabet macaroni onto the banner to spell BOO AVENUE. Glue the word BEWARE on the sign. Glue an O on the door for the doorknob. Let dry.

5 Paint the macaroni white. Shade with green. Paint doorknob orange. Let dry.

6 Glue the door, windows, and BOO AVENUE banner to one side of the pumpkin. Let dry.

7 Fold the roof piece in half. Cut an X in the center to slip over the stem. Pleat roof once on each side of fold as shown in photo, *opposite.* Place over stem.

8 Paint glitter on the stem, roof, and pumpkin. Let dry.

9 Place pumpkin in wreath. Cover wreath by poking in dried flowers. Add the BEWARE sign and miniature tree.

DOOR PATTERN

SMALL WINDOW PATTERN

LARGE WINDOW PATTERN

cinderelly's carriage

Birthday candles light
the way for this
storybook creation.

supplies
Short, wide pumpkin
Sharp knife
Spoon or ice cream
  scoop
Pencil; tracing paper
Scissors
Cardboard
Utility knife
Newspapers
Gold spray paint
Gold dimensional glitter
  paint
Gold braid
Thick white crafts glue
Upholstery tacks
Birthday cake
  candleholders
Wood disk approximately
  3 inches across
Wood heart
  approximately
  2½ inches high
2 decorative wood pegs
Small piece of gold
  fringe; matches
Birthday candles

what to do
1 Use a sharp knife
to cut a circular
shape from the top of
pumpkin. Remove the
lid. Scoop out the insides
of the pumpkin.

2 Use a pencil to draw
in arched windows
and to mark the position
of the wheels and seat.
Cut out the windows. Cut
an opening for a door on
the back of the pumpkin
if desired.

3 Trace the wheel
pattern, *page 74,* onto
tracing paper. Cut out
and trace onto cardboard
twice. Use a utility knife to
cut out the shapes.

4 In a well-ventilated
work area, cover the
work surface with
newspapers. Spray-paint
the wheels gold. Let dry.
Paint gold glitter onto
the wheels. Let dry. Glue
gold braid around each
wheel. Secure each
wheel in place with an
upholstery tack.

5 Trim all the openings
with gold braid. Hold
in place with tacks.

6 Spray-paint the
candleholders and the
wood pieces gold. Let dry.
Glue gold fringe to the
wood disk.

7 Cut an area in
pumpkin just large
enough to fit the wood
disk. Insert it into
pumpkin. Cut into

continued on page 74

pumpkin to insert the wood heart. Insert two wood pegs.

8 Insert the candleholders with candles on each side of the windows. Never leave burning candles unattended.

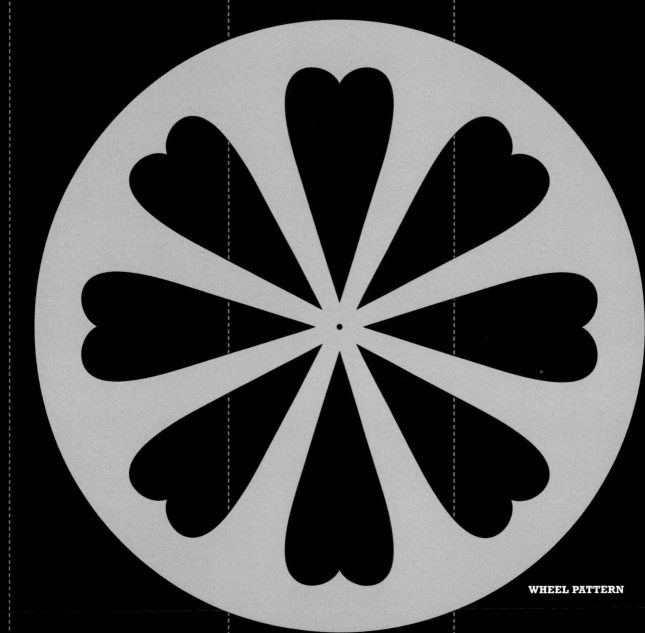

WHEEL PATTERN

partyin' pumpkin

Embellish a purchased party hat with black and orange rickrack for instant Halloween pizzazz. Make them for guests or for your favorite jack-o'-lantern.

supplies

Tape measure
Pencil
Party hat
Paper punch
Rickrack in orange and black; scissors
Hot-glue gun; glue sticks
Eyelet tool
Black eyelets
Fine gold wire
Ribbon
Pumpkin
Thick white crafts glue
Glitter

what to do

1 Measuring ½ inch from the base of the party hat, mark every inch around rim of hat. Punch holes at marks. Hot-glue a piece of black rickrack on the inside edge of the hat.

2 Secure an eyelet at each hole. Cut 12-inch lengths of rickrack. Knot one end of each length. From inside hat, thread alternating colors of rickrack through the bottom holes. Gather rickrack at the top and wrap with wire to secure at point of hat. Thread a ribbon tie through each of two opposite holes.

3 For pumpkin, draw a face with crafts glue. Sprinkle glitter over wet glue. Let dry and shake off excess glitter.

75

creepy cat

This clever black cat will bring good luck for many Halloweens to come. You'll be happy to have him cross your path or adorn your front room.

supplies

Sharp knife
Foam pumpkin
Awl; plastic animal eyes
Tracing paper; pencil
Scissors
Black marking pen
Black acrylic paint
Paintbrush
Wood-carving tools
Black craft foam
Straight pins
Ruler
Gold wire

what to do

1 Cut off the top of the pumpkin and discard the lid. Invert the pumpkin so the cut opening rests on your work surface. Trim the opening so it sits flat.

2 Poke two holes in the top front of the pumpkin and insert the plastic animal eyes through the holes.

3 Enlarge and trace the patterns, *right.* Cut out the shapes. Using a marking pen, outline the cat's body on the pumpkin. Fill in the outline with black paint. Using the photograph, *opposite,* as a guide, cut out pieces of the pumpkin to make the cat design stand out.

4 Cut two V-shape slits above the cat's eyes. Cut out black foam ears and a tail. Insert the base of the ears into the slits. Pin the cat's tail in place. Poke in 5-inch wire whiskers.

CAT FRONT PATTERN   1 SQUARE = 1 INCH

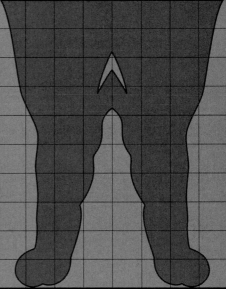

CAT BACK PATTERN   1 SQUARE = 1 INCH

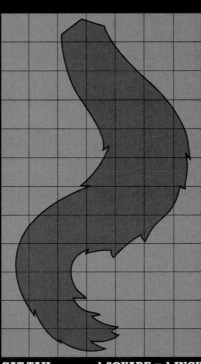

CAT TAIL PATTERN   1 SQUARE = 1 INCH

CAT EAR PATTERN 1 SQUARE = 1 INCH

77

the pumpkin keeper

A popular nursery rhyme is inscripted boldly on this carve-and-paint pumpkin.

supplies

Large pumpkin
Pencil
Knife
Scraper
Wide paint marking
  pens in purple,
  turquoise, and black
Air-dry clay, such as
  Crayola Model Magic
Acrylic paints in blue,
  white, black, orange,
  gray, and red
Paintbrush
Raffia
Straight pins
Thick white crafts glue
Foam
Drawer pull
Fencing staples
Miniature garden hoe
Candle
Matches

what to do

1 Wash and dry the pumpkin. Referring to the photograph, *opposite,* use a pencil to draw the lettering and door.

2 Cut out door shape. Cut out windowpanes. Scrape out the insides of the pumpkin.

3 Draw the words boldly using paint marking pens. Alternate the colors on each row. Define letters with a black shadow to one side and below each letter.

4 To make clay birds, shape a round head with neck and attach it to a round body shape. Form a small cone and slit it down the center for the beak. Attach to the head. Let dry. Paint birds blue, eyes white, pupils black, and beaks orange.

5 Wind a handful of raffia into a nest and place on top of pumpkin. Pin and glue nest and birds in place.

6 For the chimney, cut a rectangle from a piece of foam. Paint it gray, let dry, and paint in red bricks. Let dry. Pin in place on top of pumpkin.

7 Press drawer pull into door. Insert the ends only of two staples, one on the door and one beside the other on the pumpkin wall. Insert hoe through the staples. Place a candle in the pumpkin. Never leave burning candles unattended.

call me mr. mummy

This monster wraps guests with fear when his piercing black eyes stare at them.

supplies

Marking pen; paring
  knife
Smooth white pumpkins
Spoon or ice cream
  scoop
2 black marbles
2 flat toothpicks
Strong adhesive for
  glass, such as E6000
Candle
Matches

what to do

1 Draw a line around pumpkin top. Cut off top as shown in Photo 1, *right.* Scoop out the insides as shown in Photo 2.

2 Cut the following slits using the photograph, *opposite,* for inspiration: two for the eyes, wide and tall enough to accommodate the marbles; one for the end of the nose; and one for the mouth. Cut more slits around the pumpkin and on the edges of the lid.

3 Place a toothpick vertically into each eye opening in the pumpkin, where the marble is desired. Glue the marble to the toothpick. Let dry.

1

2

Place a candle in the pumpkin and light it. Never leave burning candles unattended.

PUMPKIN-CARVING TIPS

Protect the work surface with newspapers or a plastic tablecloth. Cut off the top or bottom of the pumpkin, cutting a small notch for easy alignment.

Scoop out the pumpkin using a sturdy spoon or ice cream scoop. Clean off the soft side of the lid as well. Carve carefully and slowly with a long, narrow, sharp knife. Special pumpkin-cutting tools are also available wherever Halloween supplies are sold.

engraved headstones

Give your guests a graven greeting with a pair of frightful pumpkins.

supplies
Sharp knife
Pumpkin
Spoon or ice cream
 scoop
Tracing paper
Pencil
Transfer paper
Wood chisel

what to do

1 Cut the pumpkin down both sides, leaving the front, back, and bottom intact. Scoop out the insides.

2 Enlarge and trace the desired pattern, *below*. Place the pattern on the pumpkin and slip a piece of transfer paper between the pumpkin and the pattern. Transfer the lines to the pumpkin.

3 Use the chisel to carve the designs into the skin of the pumpkin.

BOO PUMPKIN PATTERN   **1 SQUARE = 1 INCH**

RIP PUMPKIN PATTERN   1 SQUARE = 1 INCH

83

halloween sky

Bats take flight around this carved pumpkin with a crescent moon and dancing stars.

supplies
Sharp knife
Pumpkin
Spoon
Tracing paper
Pencil
Transfer paper
Wire screen
Scissors
Straight pins
Wire cutters
Heavyweight silver wire
Plastic bats
Candle
Matches

what to do

1 Cut off the top of the pumpkin. Scoop out.

2 Trace the star and moon patterns, *right* and *below*. Place the patterns on the pumpkin and slip transfer paper between the pumpkin and the pattern. Trace the patterns to transfer the designs. Cut out the shapes.

3 Cut the screen ½ inch larger on all sides than the moon and large stars. Push the screen into the openings. To fill smaller stars, pin a piece of screen behind each cut star on the inside of the pumpkin.

4 Cut 3-foot lengths of wire and bend them into spirals. Anchor one end of each spiral in the pumpkin and hook a bat on the other end. Never leave burning candles unattended.

STAR PATTERNS

MOON PATTERN

personal pumpkins

Haunt your house in style with these handsome monogrammed pumpkins. If you have several pumpkins, spell out greetings to welcome all visitors.

supplies
Pumpkin
Sharp knife
Spoon or ice cream scoop
Copy of monogram in desired size
Tape
Pencil
Toothpicks
Candle
Matches

what to do

1 Cut off the top of the pumpkin. Scoop out the insides.

2 Tape the copied monogram to the pumpkin surface. Lightly trace the monogram into the pumpkin flesh. Remove the paper monogram.

3 Using a knife, carefully cut out the letter. To keep center parts suspended, such as the center of the R, insert several toothpicks around the piece and replace it securely in the pumpkin. Never leave burning candles unattended.

ABCDEFGHIJ
KLMNOPQRST
UVWXYZ

clever masks

and costumes

disguises for fun and fright

cool dude masks

Get in a beach bum state of mind with these fun masks made from craft foam. Complete with brightly painted shades, keep your identity a mystery among all your surfer buddies.

supplies

Tracing paper
Pencil; scissors
2 large sheets of tan and 1 small sheet of yellow craft foam, such as Fun Foam
Adhesive for foam
Acrylic paints in light pink, dark pink, orange, yellow, and green
Paintbrush
Needle
Elastic thread
Ruler
Pierced earrings
Sunglasses
Acrylic enamel paints in desired colors
Golden marking pen

what to do

1 Enlarge and trace patterns on *pages 91–92*. Cut out. Trace patterns onto foam. Cut out.

2 Glue the pieces in place. Let dry.

3 Paint the cheeks and outer ears light pink. Paint the boy's lips light pink and the girl's dark pink. Paint orange or yellow and green accents on the hair and eyebrows. Let dry.

4 Cut a 10-inch length of elastic thread and insert into needle. Secure one end of the thread at temple area of the mask by making a small stitch and knotting the thread. Sew through opposite side of the mask, adjusting the elastic to fit. Knot thread. Trim the excess. Push earrings through earlobes.

5 Using acrylic enamel paint and a golden marking pen, make stripes on the sunglasses' frames. Let dry.

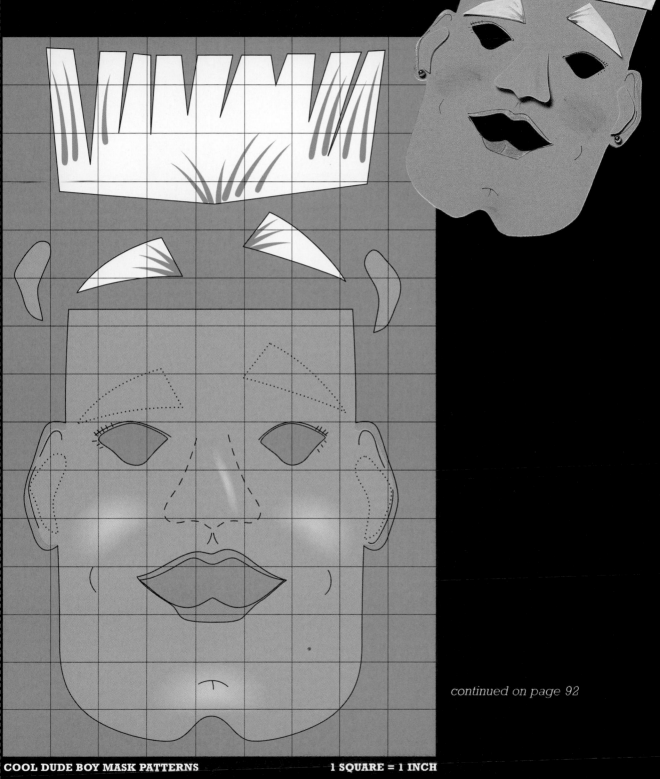

continued on page 92

COOL DUDE BOY MASK PATTERNS   **1 SQUARE = 1 INCH**

COOL DUDE GIRL MASK PATTERNS

1 SQUARE = 1 INCH

funny animal masks

Whether you want to pretend you're a pet or tweet like a bird, all of these animal masks are a hoot! Wear a coordinating sweat suit and you're ready to play the part.

fluffy and fido masks

supplies
Tracing paper
Pencil
Scissors
1 large sheet each of black and white craft foam, such as Fun Foam
1 small sheet each of tan, red, dark pink, blue, green, and yellow craft foam
Strong adhesive, such as E6000
Gem glue
Acrylic gems in purple and clear
Elastic thread; ruler
Sewing needles

what to do
1 Enlarge and trace the patterns on *pages 95–96*. Cut out the patterns. Trace around the patterns on the craft foam. Cut out the shapes.

2 Layer and glue the pieces in place. Let dry.

3 Using gem glue, adhere the gems on the cat's collar. Let dry.

4 Cut a 10-inch length of elastic thread and insert into needle. Secure one end of thread at temple area of the mask by making a small stitch and knotting the thread. Sew through opposite side of the mask, adjusting the thread to fit. Knot thread; trim.

continued on page 94

hooty owl mask

supplies

Safety goggles
(available at discount
and home center stores)
2 old CDs
Strong adhesive, such as
E6000
Tracing paper
Pencil; scissors
1 small sheet each of
black and yellow craft
foam, such as Fun
Foam; feathers

what to do

1 Put on the safety
goggles. To
determine the placement
of the CDs, look in a
mirror and place them
over the goggles,
adjusting to see in the
center holes of the CDs.
Remove from face and
glue the CDs on
the goggles.

2 Trace the patterns on
page 97. Cut out the
patterns. Trace around the
patterns on the craft foam.
Cut out the shapes.

3 Glue the foam pieces
on top of the CDs.
Using the photo, *below,* as
a guide, glue the feathers
in place. Let dry.

funny feathers mask

supplies

Tracing paper
Pencil; scissors
Craft foam in black,
white, and yellow, such
as Fun Foam
Thick white crafts glue
Eye mask
Red acrylic paint
Paintbrush
Hot-glue gun and glue
sticks; large feather

what to do

1 Trace the
patterns,
page 97. Cut out and
trace onto foam. Cut
out the shapes.

2 Use crafts glue to
adhere the white
eye pieces on the

black pieces. Lay the mask
over the foam eyes and
trace the eye holes. Cut
out the holes.

3 Paint the mask red.
Let dry.

4 Hot-glue the eyes onto
the mask, aligning the
eye holes.

5 Carefully score the
center of the beak
using scissors. Fold on the
line and glue to the mask
as shown, *below.*

6 Hot-glue the feather in
place. Let the glue dry.

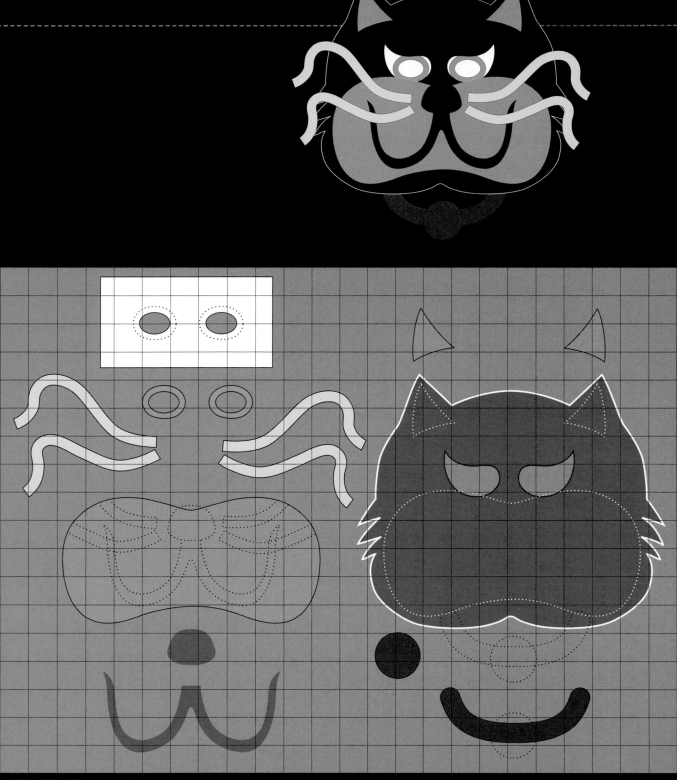

FLUFFY MASK PATTERNS

1 SQUARE = 1 INCH

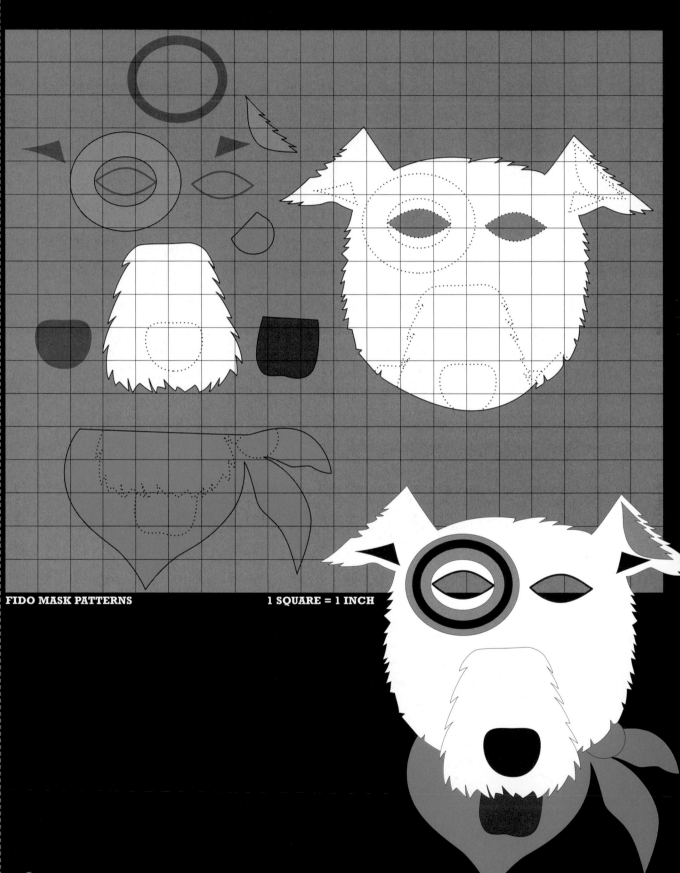

FIDO MASK PATTERNS

1 SQUARE = 1 INCH

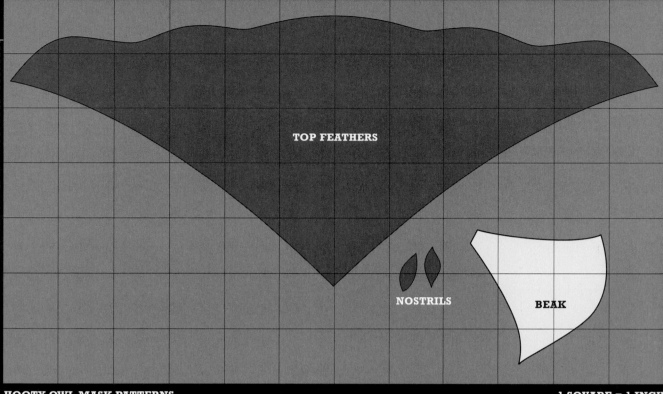

HOOTY OWL MASK PATTERNS

TOP FEATHERS

NOSTRILS

BEAK

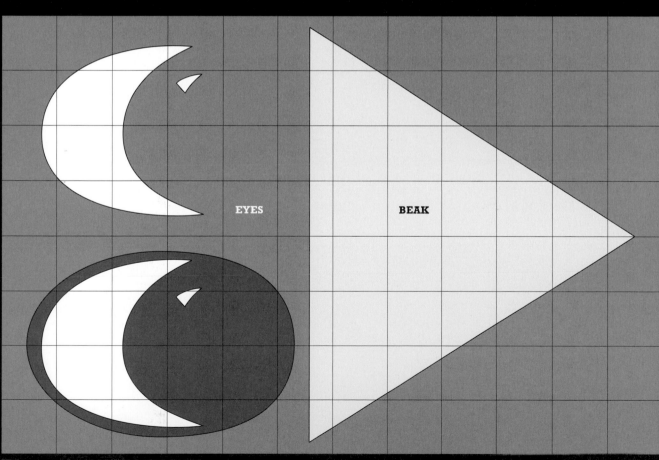

FUNNY FEATHERS MASK PATTERNS

EYES

BEAK

crazy caterpillar

For a group of young friends, this prizewinning costume gives "getting together" a whole new meaning.

Created from a length of lime green felt, the caterpillar's coat is decorated with bright, irregular spots.

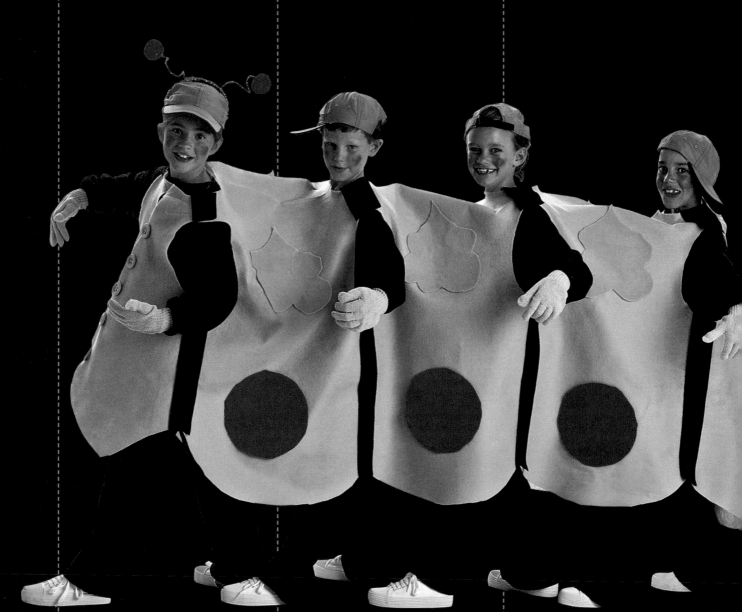

supplies
Paper; pencil
Tape measure
2½ yards of 72-inch-wide lime green felt
Scissors
Large yellow buttons
Sewing needle; thread
½ yard of 72-inch-wide black felt
Thick white crafts glue
½ yard of 72-inch-wide pink and yellow felt
Pinking shears
Tracing paper
Headband
Metallic pipe cleaners
2 large pink pom-poms
Purchased black pants and sweatshirts, white tennis shoes, and green baseball hats and gloves

what to do

1. Use paper to make an oval arm opening pattern, 12 inches high and 6 inches wide. Make a 6-inch-diameter neck opening pattern.

2. Fold green felt in half lengthwise as shown on the diagram, *page 100*. Use the patterns to mark the neck hole 4 inches from the front end at the fold. Leaving 18 inches between neck holes, mark the remaining three neck holes. Cut out the four neck holes.

3. For each arm opening, trace around the pattern 4 inches from the neck opening. Cut out the eight armholes.

4. Cut scallops across bottom from centers of armholes as shown in the diagram on *page 100*. Cut front into a vest shape and angle the back to create the look of a tail.

5. Overlap front vest pieces and secure by sewing on large buttons. Stitch back seam.

6. Cut eight 4×24-inch strips from black felt. Glue strips below armholes, trimming to match the bottom scallop.

7. Cut six 8½-inch circles from pink felt using pinking shears. Enlarge and trace the pattern, *page 101*. Use the pattern to cut six shapes from yellow felt using scissors. Glue on the cutouts as shown, *opposite*.

8. For antennae, wrap pipe cleaners around a headband. Glue pom-poms to ends of two pipe cleaners and twist around sides of headband. Place over the hat of the leader. Dress four kids in matching purchased clothes and put on costume.

continued on page 100

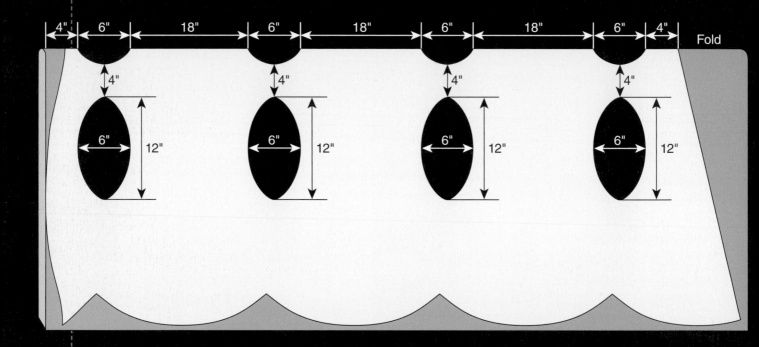

CATERPILLAR DIAGRAM

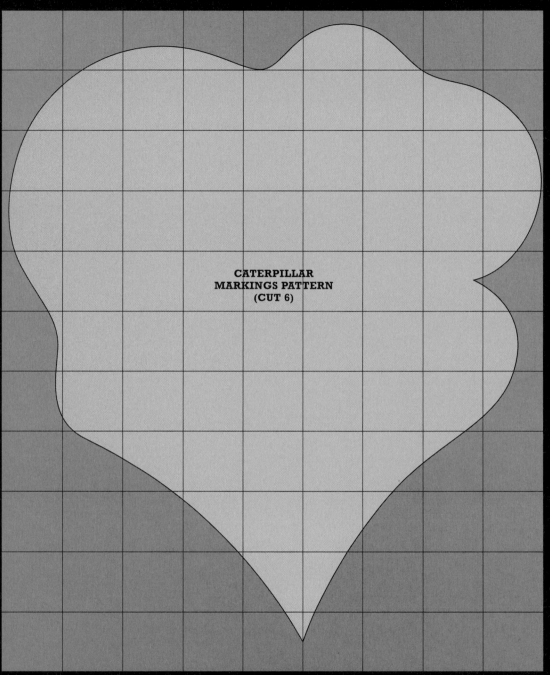

CATERPILLAR
MARKINGS PATTERN
(CUT 6)

1 SQUARE = 1 INCH

Look like the queen of Egypt herself with this golden costume embellished with gems of all colors. An elegant golden doily, dripping with beads, provides the crowning touch.

supplies
Scissors
3 yards of 45-inch-wide metallic knit fabric with sequins
Thread; sewing needle
Tape measure
Two 9-inch pieces of $\frac{1}{2}$-inch-wide elastic
1 yard of 45-inch-wide quilted golden lamé
4 yards of $\frac{1}{2}$-inch-wide sequin trim
Fabric glue
Assorted acrylic gems
Gem glue
1 yard of $\frac{1}{4}$-inch-wide grosgrain ribbon
Tracing paper
Pencil
$1\frac{1}{4}$ yards of 4-inch-wide sequined elastic
4 yards of golden beads on a string
8-inch-diameter golden crocheted doily
1 yard of 2-inch-wide sequined elastic
Sandals
Glitter face paint

what to do

1 Cut an 8-inch neck opening in the center of the metallic knit fabric. Fold the fabric piece in half, right sides together, with the short ends meeting. Sew the side seams, allowing 10-inch arm openings and 10-inch bottom slits on both sides. Turn.

2 Along each shoulder, stretch and stitch a 9-inch piece of elastic to the inside of the garment.

3 For collar, use the diagram on *page 104* as a guide to cut a 17-inch-diameter circle from lamé. Cut a 5-inch-diameter circle in the center for neck opening. Cut center back open. Topstitch a narrow hem around all edges. Glue the sequin trim to collar edge. Adhere gems to the collar where desired. Stitch ribbons to each corner of the center back opening for ties.

4 For belt apron, enlarge and trace pattern from *page 105*. Cut the shape from lamé. Glue the trim and gems to the belt apron as shown in the photographs, *above.* Cut the 4-inch-wide sequined elastic to a comfortable waist measurement plus seams. Stitch the apron to the center front of 4-inch-wide sequined elastic belt. Stitch center back seam of belt.

5 For headpiece, cut the beaded string into 10 equal pieces. Sew five to each side of doily as shown, *opposite.* Glue on gems as desired. Let the glue dry.

6 To make upper arm bands, cut 2-inch-wide sequined elastic two inches larger than upper arm measurement. Sew a 1-inch seam, tacking ends to back of elastic. Wear sandals and decorate face with glitter face paint.

continued on page 104

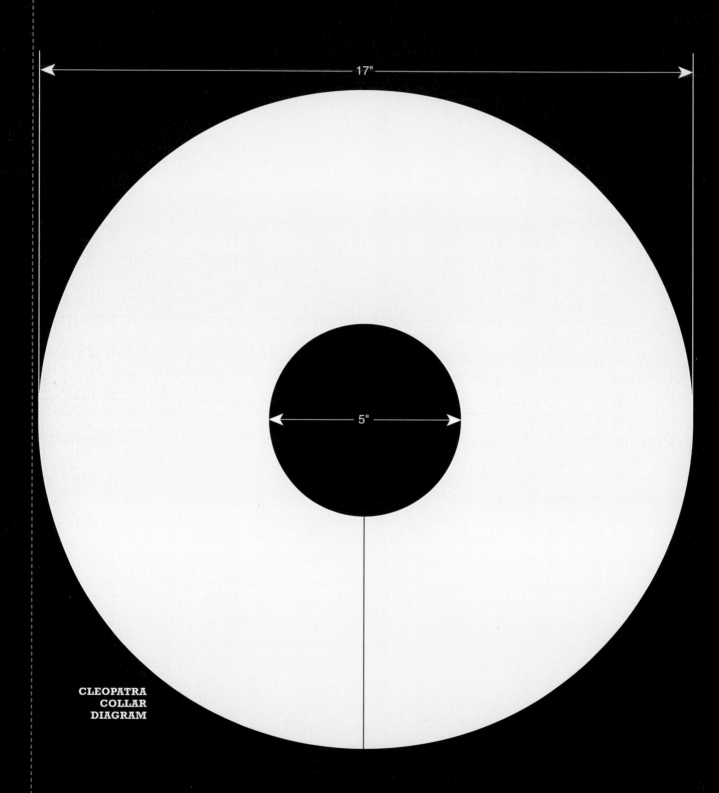

17"

5"

**CLEOPATRA
COLLAR
DIAGRAM**

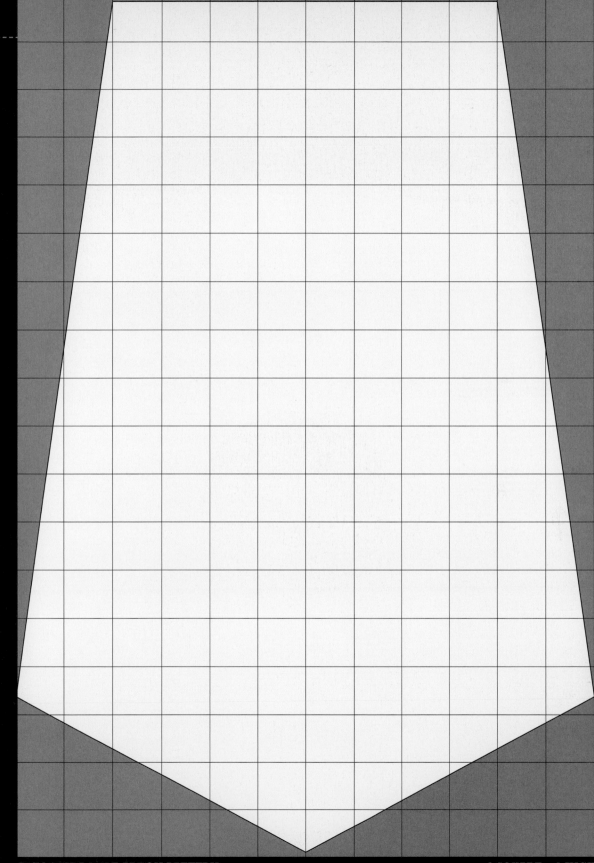

CLEOPATRA BELT APRON PATTERN

from a recycled box.

   Or create a caveman
with fake fur and
spray paint.

squeaky the mouse

supplies

For costume:
Tracing paper
Pencil
Scissors
$\frac{1}{3}$ yard gray felt
9×12-inch piece of
   pink felt
Thick white crafts glue
Pipe cleaner
Stapler
1 yard pink baby
   rickrack
White plastic headband
Hot-glue gun and
   glue sticks
Small natural sponge
White acrylic paint
Gray hooded sweat suit

For face paint:
1 teaspoon cornstarch
½ teaspoon cold cream
Bowl; spoon
½ teaspoon water
Muffin pan
Food coloring
**Small paintbrush or
  cotton swab**

what to do

1 Enlarge and trace the mouse ear patterns, *right,* and cut out. Cut two outer ears from gray felt. Cut two inner ears from pink felt.

2 Glue an inner ear onto each outer ear, sandwiching half a pipe cleaner between. Tuck each ear, securing with a staple along the bottom edge. Glue rickrack around the outer edge of each inner ear.

3 Cut a strip of gray felt the length and width of the headband. Glue the strip along the top of the headband, trimming as necessary to match the edges. Bend the bottom 1 inch of each ear forward at a 90-degree angle. Hot-glue the bent portion of each ear to the underside of the headband.

4 Dip a moist sponge into a puddle of white paint; sponge-paint the gray on the ears and headband. Let dry.

5 For face paint, stir together the cornstarch and cold cream in a bowl until it is well-blended. Add water and stir.

6 Decide how many colors of paint you want. Put a dab of the cold cream mixture into a muffin pan for each color. Mix in food coloring, one drop at a time, until the colors are achieved. Mix well.

7 Using the photograph, *opposite,* for inspiration, paint the cheeks and nose using a paintbrush or cotton swab. Paint whiskers and other details as desired.

flying high airplane

supplies
**Cardboard box
  appropriate for the size
  of the child**
Duct tape; utility knife
Tracing paper; pencil
**Extra flat pieces of
  cardboard**
**Hot-glue gun and
  glue sticks; ruler**
Plastic margarine tub
Newspapers

continued on page 108

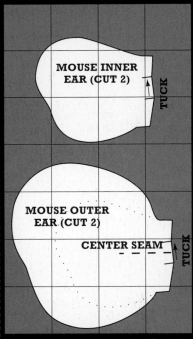

MOUSE INNER
EAR (CUT 2)

TUCK

MOUSE OUTER
EAR (CUT 2)

CENTER SEAM

TUCK

**SQUEAKY
THE MOUSE
PATTERNS**

**1 SQUARE =
2 INCHES**

107

Spray paint in desired
color
4×4×1-inch piece of wood
Drill and drill bit
Bolt slightly longer than
margarine tub depth
and a nut
Colored electrical tape
Two 30-inch-long pieces
of 1½-inch fabric
strapping

what to do

1 Fold flaps from the
box bottom to the
inside and tape in place.
Fold the two side flaps
from the top to the inside
and tape in place. Using
a utility knife, trim
semicircles from the two
remaining flaps to allow a
child to stand in the box.

2 Enlarge and trace the
plane patterns,
opposite. Cut the shapes
from cardboard.

3 Use hot-glue to attach
the tail top to the
center of the tail. Glue the
two tail supports
perpendicular to the
underside of the tail, each
about 2 inches from the
center. Glue two supports
to the underside of each
wing, aligning with the
outside edge as shown in
the photo on *page 106.*
With straight sides
aligned, glue the
propellers to the

propeller center. Glue the
propeller unit to the
bottom of the margarine
tub. Let all glue set.

4 In a well-ventilated
area, cover your work
surface with newspapers.
Spray-paint all sides of the
box and cardboard
pieces. Let the paint dry.

5 Assemble the airplane
using hot-glue
according to the
photograph, *page 106.* To
add the propeller, back it
with the wood square
inside the box. Drill a hole
through the box and wood
piece. Drill a hole in the
center of the propeller.
Secure in place with a nut
and bolt.

6 Form stripes on the
airplane using
electrical tape.

7 Cut two 1½-inch-long
slits in each untaped
box flap for shoulder
straps. Insert the ends of
the strapping through the
slits. Adjust to fit child
and knot the ends of the
strapping.

tough-guy caveman

supplies

Spray paint in black,
gray, and brown
⅞ yard of 60-inch-wide
gray fake fur

Scissors; gray thread
Sewing needle
Three 1-yard-long strips
of brown leather
Vinyl dog bone
Fat baseball bat
Newspapers
Masking tape
Sandals

what to do

1 Spray-paint fake fur
with stripes of gray
and black as desired. Let
the paint dry.

2 Cut a straight tunic
front and back from
painted fur. Cut a
diamond shape in the
center for the neck. Stitch
side seams from bottom
edge, leaving 10 inches
open for each arm.
Cut jagged points into
the bottom.

3 For necklace, tie the
center of one leather
strip around one end of
the bone. Knot ends.

4 For arm bands, tie
leather strips in
crisscross fashion around
the upper arms. Tie ends.

5 For club, pad bat with
crumpled newspapers.
Secure in place with
masking tape. Wrap the
entire bat with tape,
covering the papers.
Spray the club with
gray and brown paint.
Wear sandals.

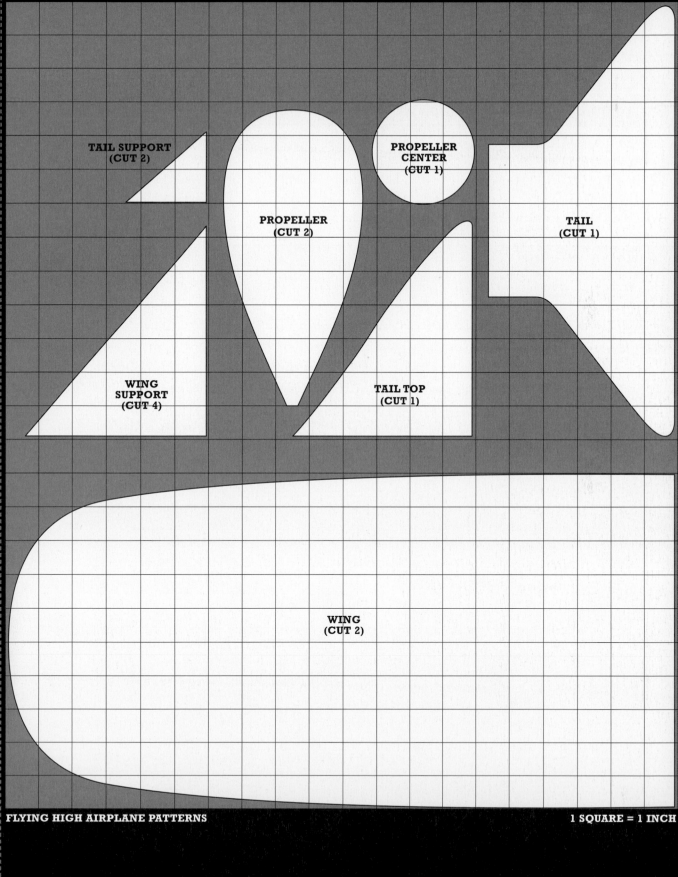

TAIL SUPPORT
(CUT 2)

PROPELLER
(CUT 2)

PROPELLER
CENTER
(CUT 1)

TAIL
(CUT 1)

WING
SUPPORT
(CUT 4)

TAIL TOP
(CUT 1)

WING
(CUT 2)

FLYING HIGH AIRPLANE PATTERNS

1 SQUARE = 1 INCH

lulu the ladybug

Here's a last-minute costume idea that's cute as a bug! Wings made of craft foam and a purchased hat embellished with pipe cleaner and pom-pom antennae transform any little munchkin into a fun-loving lulu of a ladybug.

supplies
Pencil
Tracing paper
Scissors
**¼-inch-thick red
  craft foam**
Thin black craft foam
**Hot-glue gun and
  glue sticks**
Paper punch
4 eyelets and eyelet tool
**Pair of 42-inch-long black
  shoelaces**
Purchased red hat
Black pipe cleaner
2 large black pom-poms
**Purchased black gloves,
  shirt, and pants**

what to do
1 Enlarge and trace the wing and dot patterns, *page 113,* onto tracing paper. Cut out. Cut two wings from red foam and six dots from the black foam.

2 Using the diagram, *page 112,* glue the short straight edges of the wings together. Glue three dots on each wing. Let the glue dry.

3 Use a paper punch to make two holes at the top of each wing. For reinforcement, insert an eyelet in each.

4 Tie the shoelaces together at one end. Place the knot by the seam on the wrong side of the wings. Thread the laces through the holes in each wing.

5 For hat, poke a pipe cleaner through the top of the hat. Glue a pom-pom on each end. Let dry. Dress in black clothing and put on hat and wings.

continued on page 112

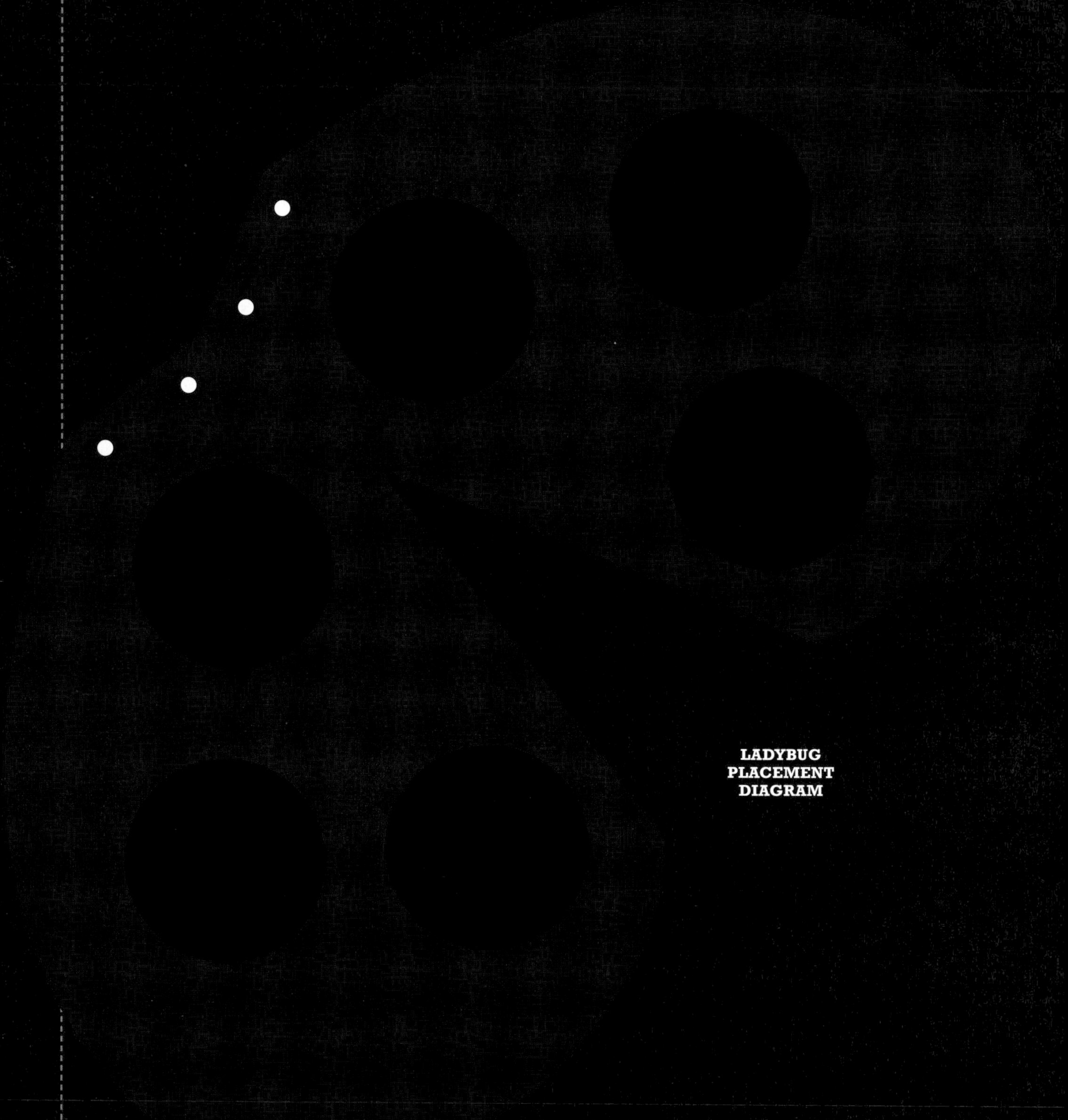

**LADYBUG
PLACEMENT
DIAGRAM**

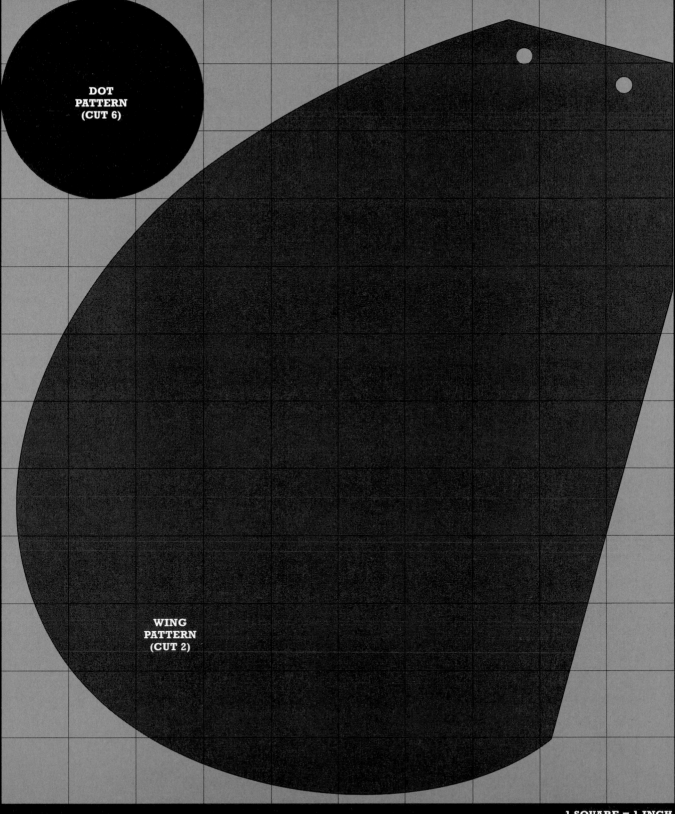

DOT
PATTERN
(CUT 6)

WING
PATTERN
(CUT 2)

1 SQUARE = 1 INCH

clarise the clown

Get ready to put on a happy face with this cheerful clown costume. Bright fabrics and rickrack turn an ordinary sweat suit into circuslike attire.

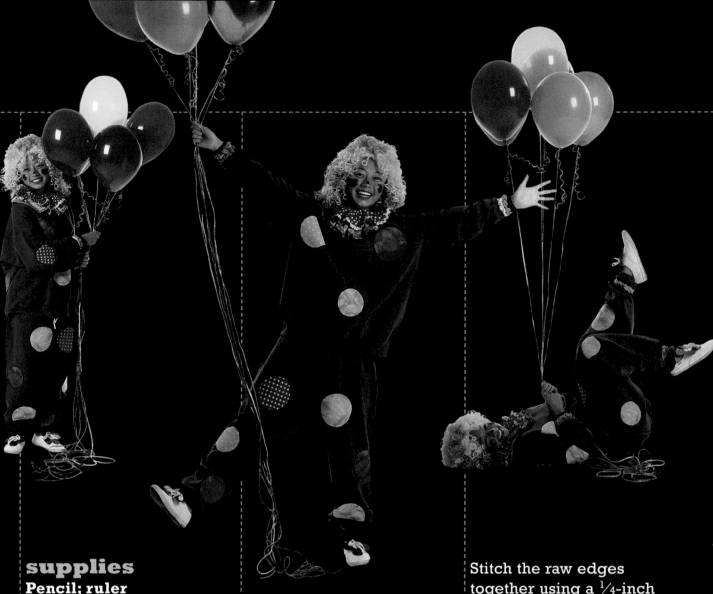

supplies

Pencil; ruler
Fusible web paper
Assorted bright solid
  and polka-dot fabrics
Scissors
Blue sweat suit
Thread; sewing needle
4×72-inch piece of
  bright fabric
5×72-inch piece of
  coordinating bright
  fabric
2 yards each of jumbo
  rickrack in two colors
1 yard of ³⁄₈-inch-wide
  grosgrain ribbon; iron
Purchased wig
Hair bands for cuffs
Face paints

what to do

1 Draw 4- and
5-inch-diameter
circles onto web paper.
Fuse to bright fabrics.
Cut out the fabric pieces
and fuse to the sweatsuit.

2 To make the collar,
stitch a narrow hem
on two short ends and one
long side of each bright
fabric rectangle. Topstitch
rickrack to each of the
long hemmed edges.
Layer the narrow strip on
the wide strip with the
right sides facing up.

Stitch the raw edges
together using a ¹⁄₄-inch
seam allowance. Press the
seam open.

3 Gather along the seam
to about 18 inches.
Stitch the gathered edge
onto the ribbon. Tie the
collar around the neck.
Put on wig, wrap hair
bands around wrists, and
paint face.

all abuzz suits

Set your neighborhood abuzz when everyone sees your little one in these bold stripes. The tabard pattern could be easily enlarged for a matching adult version.

If you have only minutes to spare, make the cute frog getup, opposite. Just attach the eyes and neck detail to a sweat suit.

beatrice bee

supplies
Tracing paper
Pencil; scissors
24×48-inch piece of heavy sew-in interfacing
3 yards of 72-inch-wide black felt
¼ yard of 72-inch-wide yellow felt; spray adhesive; tape measure
Thick white crafts glue
6 yards of medium yellow rickrack
3 black loopy pipe cleaners
Black headband
Two 2-inch yellow pom-poms
Yellow gloves

what to do
1 Enlarge and trace patterns, *right.* Cut two tabards from interfacing and four from black felt. Cut two stingers from yellow felt.

2 Layer the interfacing tabards between felt tabards, using spray adhesive to temporarily secure layers. Machine-zigzag-stitch around neck and outer edges.

3 Cut six 3×22-inch yellow felt strips. Glue strips to tabard as indicated on pattern. Trim ends to match tabard. Glue yellow rickrack around neck and outer edges.

Stitch an 18-inch-long piece of yellow rickrack to each side at the X to make ties.

4 Glue stinger points together, sandwiching one end of a pipe cleaner between. Stitch remaining end of pipe cleaner to dot on tabard back.

5 For antennae, twist one end of each remaining pipe cleaner around top of headband. Glue a pom-pom to each tip. Let dry.

ready-to-leap frog

supplies
Scissors; ruler
¼ yard green felt
Fabric glue
Green hooded sweat suit, gloves, and swim fins
2 table tennis balls
Permanent black marking pen

what to do
1 Cut nine 6-inch-long triangles from green felt. With narrow points down, glue around sweatshirt below hood. Let dry.

2 Cut two 4×7-inch pieces from felt. Align the center of one long edge with the center of a table tennis ball. Shape

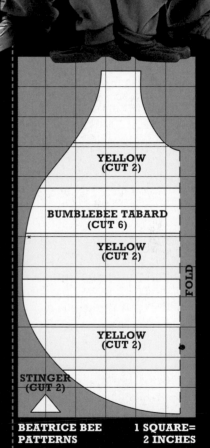

BEATRICE BEE PATTERNS   **1 SQUARE= 2 INCHES**

YELLOW (CUT 2)
BUMBLEBEE TABARD (CUT 6)
YELLOW (CUT 2)
FOLD
YELLOW (CUT 2)
STINGER (CUT 2)

and glue felt to ball at top and sides. Let dry.

3 Draw a dime-size dot in the middle of each table tennis ball. Draw a slanted 1-inch-long line through each dot.

4 Glue the eyes to top of the hood. Let dry.

magic tree costume

As glorious as those from Mother Nature, this realistic tree exhibits barklike fleece, artificial foliage, nests, and butterflies.

supplies
1 yard of textured fur or bark-patterned fleece
Child's T-shirt for pattern
Scissors; tape measure
1 yard of quilted backing
Pins; thread
Sewing needle
4 feet of ribbon
Hot-glue gun and glue sticks
1 sheet of brown craft foam, such as Fun Foam
Feathered monarch butterflies
4 artificial autumn foliage bushes
7-inch-long piece of ribbon
Hook-and-loop tape
Straw hat
Moss
2 artificial bird's nests, 4 bird eggs, and birds

what to do

1 To make the tree trunk vest, fold the fleece in half. Lay your child's T-shirt over the folded fabric to serve as a pattern. Cut the fabric $1\frac{1}{2}$ inches from the side and shoulder seams of the T-shirt. The bottom of the front is cut shorter than the back. Make a V-neckline by cutting triangular shapes from neck. Cut two quilted backing pieces: one to match the tree front and one to match the back. Place the right side of the quilted backing over the right side of its matching fur piece and pin together. Sew around the edge of each set, leaving a 12-inch opening along the side seam. Trim away any excess fabric and turn both vest pieces right side out. Lay the finished front over the finished back, matching right sides together. Pin the side seams together and then stitch through

the four layers of fabric. Sew one end of a 12-inch length of ribbon to each shoulder. The ribbons tie together over the shoulder after the vest is pulled over the child's head. Hot-glue small strips of brown craft foam and feathered butterflies to the finished trunk and glue small sections of foliage around the vest neck.

2 To make the wristbands, cut two quilted strips 7×3 inches long. Lay them right side down on the work surface. Fold the entire length of the top and bottom edges of each strip $\frac{1}{2}$ inch into the center. Hot-glue

these folds in place and hot-glue a 7-inch length of ribbon along the center of each band, trapping the folded edges and covering the remaining wrong side of the quilted backing. Cut four 2-inch lengths of ribbon and then fold one over each end of the wristband. Hot-glue them in place so they neatly cover the fabric ends. Glue a 2-inch section of hook-and-loop tape to each end of the wristbands. Trim the wristbands by gluing foliage and butterflies onto the right side of the finished bands.

3 To make the hat, hot-glue pieces of moss to the underside, outer edge, and top of the hat brim. Cut branches of foliage off the bushes and glue to hat. Continue gluing branches and moss until the hat is disguised. Position the nests, eggs, and birds onto the branches. Glue in place.

119

milky milk shake

Bring out your bubbly personality with this fun milk shake costume. Made from metallic vinyl, the drinking glass is supported by a plastic laundry basket. The balloon bubbles and striped mailing-tube straw complete this silly Halloween wear.

supplies

63×40-inch piece of metallic vinyl (available in the upholstery section of fabric stores)

Pencil

Ruler

Scissors

Round plastic laundry basket

Hot-glue gun and glue sticks

Shoelaces or ribbons

White mailing tube

1-inch-wide bright pink ribbon

Clear and white balloons

Curling ribbon

what to do

1 On the back side of the vinyl, draw a line 2 inches from one long edge. On the same long edge, draw a line every 3½ inches from the edge of the vinyl to the 2-inch mark. Cut along these markings.

2 Cut the bottom out of the laundry basket. Leaving the top rim intact, cut holes on opposite sides for armholes.

3 With the clipped edge at the top, wrap the vinyl piece around the basket to form a drinking glass. Hot-glue the clipped edge to the inside of the basket rim. Leave the back seam open so the person wearing the costume can sit down. Cut round armholes in the

vinyl at the laundry basket holes.

4 Tie the shoelaces or ribbons to the inside of the basket for shoulder straps. Try on the costume and adjust as necessary.

5 To make the straw, hot-glue one bright pink ribbon end to the inside edge of the mailing tube. Wrap ribbon diagonally around the tube to create a continuous stripe. Cut the ribbon. Glue the end inside the tube.

6 For bubbles, inflate several balloons. Tie the balloons to the top of the costume with curling ribbon.

ghostly jewelry

Get in the Halloween spirit with these gliding ghosts that would rather hang out with you than rattle any chains.

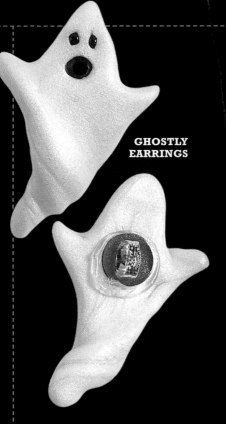

GHOSTLY EARRINGS

GHOSTLY NECKLACE

supplies

Pearlescent white polymer clay
Flat-back black rhinestones
Black seed beads
Darning needle or toothpick
Narrow black leather cord
Earring backs
Strong adhesive, such as E6000

what to do

1 Work the clay in your hands to make it warm and pliable. Form a ghost with a ¾-inch diameter ball of clay. Pinch the top into a flat, rounded point; then pinch out two small arms from the sides. Flatten the center and then lengthen the remaining clay to end in a point. Twist the point under and around to give the bottom a swirling effect.

2 Press a rhinestone mouth and seed bead eyes in place. For necklace pieces, pierce a darning needle or toothpick sideways through the top of the ghost to make holes for stringing.

3 Bake according to package instructions. Thread pierced ghosts onto the leather cord, tying knots in the cord to separate the ghosts. Glue remaining ghosts to earring backs. Let the glue dry.

jesting jester

You can't help but feel jolly with this jingling jester in your midst. The hat and collar are made from bright felt and the polka-dot stick has trailing ribbons with jingle-bell ends.

supplies
Tracing paper
Pencil with round eraser
Scissors
Felt in turquoise, yellow, orange, bright pink, black, and purple
Pinking shears
Matching thread
Sewing needle; buttons
Fiberfill; jingle bells
Straight pins
Child's sweatshirt
Purple cotton embroidery floss
23-inch length of ¾-inch dowel
2-inch wood doll head
Hot-glue gun; glue sticks
Acrylic paints in orange and black; paintbrush
2 yards of 1-inch-wide black and orange wire-edge ribbon

what to do
1 Enlarge and trace the patterns on

pages 126–127. Cut out the patterns. Use the patterns to cut pieces from felt with pinking shears.

2 To make the hat, layer the front and the back pieces. Using ¼-inch seams, sew the front and back sets together. Sew the left and right top pieces together. For the hatband, cut a 21×2½-inch piece from yellow felt. Sew the short ends together. Sew the band to the top piece. Sew buttons where indicated on the pattern. Stuff the points of the hat with fiberfill. Sew a jingle bell on each point.

3 To make the collar, pin the felt pieces in place, using the photo, *opposite,* as a guide. Sew the felt pieces to the sweatshirt around the collar area with embroidery floss and small Xs. Tack the tips down by sewing a jingle bell to each tip.

4 To make the stick, glue the flat side of the wood doll head to one end of the dowel. Paint the dowel orange and the doll head black. Let the paint dry. To make polka dots, dip the eraser of a pencil into the paint and dot onto

the surface. Let the paint dry. Cut the ribbon in half. Tie one ribbon length just below the doll head on the stick. Knot in place. Tie the remaining ribbon above the first, tying the ends into a bow. To string a jingle bell on each ribbon end, pull both wires in each ribbon end to extend 1 inch beyond the ribbon. Twist the ends together. Insert the twisted wires into the loop in a jingle bell. Twist to secure.

continued on page 126

JESTER COLLAR PATTERN

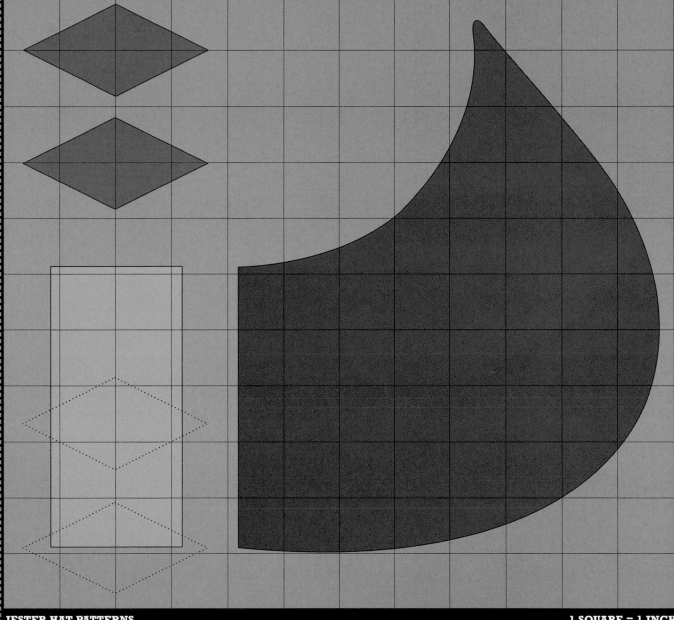

127

fancy flapper

Dance your way back to the 1920s with this flashy little number.

supplies

- 2 tab-top curtain panels with decorative bottom
- Scissors
- Thread
- Sewing needle
- Elastic sequin trim
- Feathers
- Purchased boa, long gloves, jewelry, and fishnet stockings

what to do

1 Cut off the tabs from the curtain tops. Fold one piece in half lengthwise. Allowing for desired width, cut out rounded underarm shapes. Repeat for the dress back.

2 Stitch side seam, leaving a slit at the bottom edge. Stitch elastic sequin trim around armholes and along the front and the back of the bodice, stretching the trim as it is stitched.

3 For the headband, stitch a length of elastic sequin trim into the desired size loop. Stitch feathers to the sequin trim.

4 Accessorize costume with a purchased boa, long gloves, jewelry, and fishnet stockings.

fold

DRESS DIAGRAM

bootiful bat

No one will fear this nocturnal nymph although it has a wingspan larger than any bat around.

supplies

60-inch square of black fabric
White sewing pencil
Scissors; fusible facing
Tape measure
Elastic; sequin trim in silver and red
Thread; sewing needle
Black buttons
Purchased black sweatshirt, black leggings or sweatpants, bat ears, white gloves, and plastic fangs

what to do

1 Fold the fabric in half to form a triangle. Using the photograph, *above,* for inspiration, draw lines for the wings.

2 Cut out the wings through both layers using the diagram, *right,* for inspiration. Cut out a center circle for the neck. Adjust size of cape at the arms and head opening according to the child.

3 Fuse facing inside the neck opening. Make small slits in neck facing about 1½ inches apart. Thread elastic through the slits; adjust to fit.

4 For trim, stitch a single row of silver sequin trim along each line in the wing front and back. Stitch red sequin trim around the bottom edge.

5 Fit cape wings on the child. Sew two sets of black buttons at the underarm through both layers to secure the cape on the arms.

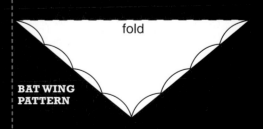

fold

BAT WING PATTERN

129

little red riding hood

With a basket for goody getting, this little costume wins oodles of smiles.

supplies
Measuring tape
Scissors
Round red plaid
tablecloth
Fusible hem tape
Elastic
3¼ yards pre-gathered
lace
Red fabric or flat sheet
Ruffled red trim
Red sport weight yarn
Red ribbon
White blouse
Basket

what to do

1 For skirt, measure waist. Make a circle pattern the same circumference as the waist measurement. Cut out circle from center of tablecloth. Trim tablecloth if necessary to shorten.

2 Use fusible hem tape to press under 1 inch of raw edge at waist, clipping as necessary. Make small slits in waistline hem about 1½ inches apart. Thread elastic through the slits; adjust to fit waist. Sew lace around bottom hem.

3 For cape, measure from back of neck downward to determine length. Fold fabric in half so center back of cape is on fold. Draw a curve to make a quarter circle. Cut out a rounded neckline. Use diagram, *right,* to draw hood portion of cape; cut out.

4 Stitch ruffled red trim at edge of hood. With yarn, make a gathering stitch at bottom of hood where indicated on diagram; secure at sides.

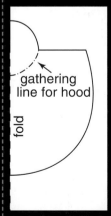

gathering line for hood

fold

HOODED CAPE DIAGRAM

bone bangles

Before you head out to your next ghostly gala, put on this rattling set of skeleton bones. Wear them around your neck and your wrist—they're the perfect costume jewelry for every costume party!

supplies
Pearl white polymer clay, such as Premo Sculpey or Granitex
Silver eye pins
Small wire cutters
Silver jump rings
Needlenose pliers
Silver T- and O-clasps

what to do

1 Mold ½- to ¾-inch bones out of polymer clay. Insert an eye pin into both ends of each bone so that only the circular eyes extend beyond the end of the bone. You will need to trim many of the eye pins with wire cutters before inserting them into the bones.

2 Bake the bones according to the clay manufacturer's instructions.

3 To join the bones, use needlenose pliers to make a small gap in the jump ring. Hook two bone ends onto the ring and then carefully use the pliers to close the jump ring. Connect enough bones to make a bracelet or necklace. Attach an extra jump ring on both ends of the bone chain to connect both the T- and O-clasps.

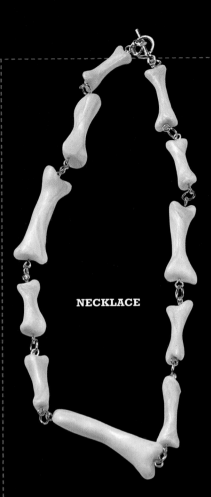

NECKLACE

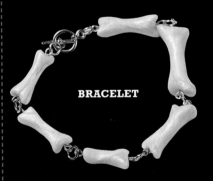

BRACELET

awesome toppers

black and orange hat

supplies
Tracing paper
Pencil
Scissors
Heavy orange paper
Black paper
Black glitter paint
Orange fabric paint
Double-stick tape
Thick white crafts glue
Black pipe cleaners
Orange beads

what to do
1 Enlarge and trace the hat patterns on *page 137,* cut out, and transfer onto orange and black papers as shown in photo, *right.* Cut out.

2 Use black glitter paint to draw random coil shapes on the orange paper. Let dry. Paint orange wavy lines down the center of the black strips.

3 Place a piece of double-stick tape down one edge of orange paper and shape the paper into a cone.

4 Use a dab of glue to affix the black strips to the top and bottom of

continued on page 136

Put on any of these
Halloween hats and
you are ready to
party until the bats
come home!

hat. Fold a small tip of the narrow end and insert into the tip of cone and glue.

5 Put assorted orange beads onto ends of pipe cleaners and insert into the tip of the hat with a small dab of glue.

eyeball hat

supplies

Tracing paper
Pencil
Scissors
Heavy green paper
Purple stretch fleece fabric; ruler
Green felt
Double-stick tape
Spray adhesive
Plastic eyeballs
Two 1½-inch plastic foam balls, such as Styrofoam
Orange acrylic paint
Paintbrush
Thick white crafts glue
Pipe cleaner

what to do

1 Enlarge and trace the hat pattern (without the spiderweb design), *opposite,* and cut out. Trace onto both green paper and purple fabric. Cut out. Draw a 4-inch-long triangle on tracing paper and cut out. Trace about six triangles onto green felt and cut out.

2 Shape the paper into a cone and secure with double-stick tape.

3 Spray a coat of adhesive to the outside of the green paper hat.

4 Attach the eyeballs randomly in pairs.

5 Wrap the purple fabric around the hat, aligning the shape and covering the eyeballs. The fleece should stick to the adhesive on the paper. Place a strip of double-stick tape at the seam if needed.

6 Feeling the eyeballs through the fabric, cut small horizontal slits in the fabric over the eyeballs.

7 Paint the foam balls with acrylic paint. Let dry. Glue on eyeballs with crafts glue. Let dry.

8 Bend a pipe cleaner in half and insert a foam ball on each end. Insert and glue folded end of pipe cleaner into tip of hat.

9 Glue triangles onto the bottom edge of hat, overlapping each other.

spider hat

supplies

Tracing paper; pencil
Scissors
Heavy black paper
Utility knife
White paint pen
Double-stick tape
8 orange wavy pipe cleaners
Thick white crafts glue
2-inch foam ball, such as Styrofoam
Orange acrylic paint
Paintbrush; 2 plastic eyes
Orange ribbon

what to do

1 Trace hat pattern, *opposite,* onto tracing paper, cut out, and trace onto black paper. Cut out black hat shape.

2 Use a utility knife to very lightly score along vertical web lines as shown on pattern. Draw in web lines using a white paint pen. Let dry.

3 Run a piece of double-stick tape along one edge of hat, coil into a cone, and affix ends together.

4 Twist eight orange wavy pipe cleaners together at one end and insert that end into the tip

of the hat. Place a dab of glue for extra support. Bend pipe cleaners into spider legs.

5 Paint foam ball orange and let dry. Glue onto top center of hat. Glue eyes onto foam ball.

6 Make hat ties using orange ribbon.

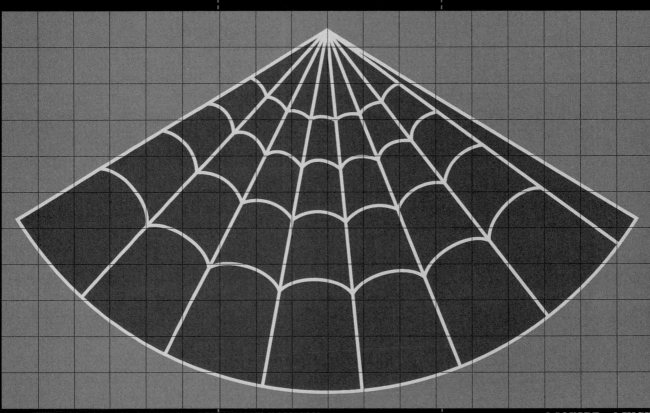

HAT PATTERN FOR ALL HATS AND SPIDERWEB PATTERN

1 SQUARE = 1 INCH

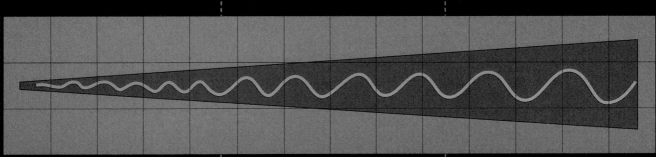

BLACK AND ORANGE HAT PATTERN

1 SQUARE = 1 INCH

hazel and broomhilda

After parking their brooms at the door, these witty witches are thirsting for some party brew. With such easy-to-make skirts and capes, they can be transformed into witches in the blink of a cat's eye.

supplies

Tape measure
Pencil; scissors
70-inch round tablecloth
 for adult skirt
60-inch round tablecloth
 for youth skirt
Fusible hem tape
Elastic; interfacing
1 yard of black fabric or
 round tablecloth*
Pinking shears
Ribbon; button
Purchased shirts and
 hats

what to do

1 For each skirt, measure the waist of the person who will be wearing the costume. Make a circle pattern the same circumference as the waist measurement. Cut out this circle from the tablecloth center.

2 Use fusible hem tape to press under 1 inch of raw edge at waist, clipping as necessary to make pressing easy. Make small slits in waistline hem about 1½ inches apart. Thread elastic through the slits; adjust to fit waist.

3 For cape, measure from back of neck downward to determine length. Fold fabric in half so center back of cape is on fold. Draw a curve to make a quarter circle. Cut out a rounded neckline. If using a tablecloth to make capes, cut in half and cut out rounded necklines.

4 Fuse interfacing or fabric around neck edge about 2 inches wide. Trim neck and bottom edges with pinking shears. Fringe the bottom edge with straight scissors.

5 Make ½-inch slits approximately 1 inch apart in neck facing. Thread ribbon through slits, ending with ribbon on the right side. Gather slightly. Sew a button on ribbon through cape to secure gathers. Wear purchased hats and shirts.

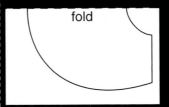

CAPE DIAGRAM

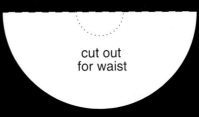

SKIRT DIAGRAM

*Note: *Look in the linen department for tablecloths, flat panel curtains, sheets, and shower curtains. When making a cape, cut with front edge on hem by folding panel crosswise. Shower curtains and sheets provide wide pieces of fabric with no seams. Round tablecloths make one skirt or two capes.*

haunting

eeriesistible ideas to scare them silly

decorations

Round glass
ornaments transform
quickly into a gathering
of Halloween trims.
Hung from fallen
branches that are
spray-painted purple,
these ornaments
celebrate the holiday
with style. The
instructions for all the
ornaments begin on
page 146.

halloween tree trims

JACK-O'-LANTERN ORNAMENT

HALLOWEEN SWIRL ORNAMENT

POLKA-DOT ORNAMENTS

STARRY NIGHT ORNAMENT

SPIDER-'N'-WEB ORNAMENT

**BOO-TO-YOU
ORNAMENT**

polka-dot ornaments

supplies
Round purple or
green ornaments
Newspapers; string
Glass paints in black,
orange, yellow, purple,
and green
Disposable plate
Pencil with round eraser
Clear iridescent glitter,
if desired
Toothpick or paintbrush
5 inches of lime green
sequins on a string
Thick white crafts glue
1/8- to 1/4-inch-wide
ribbon

what to do
1 Wash and dry the
ornaments. Avoid
touching the areas to
be painted.
2 Cover the work
surface with
newspapers. Tie a
temporary string hanger
onto each ornament.
3 Place desired paint
colors on a plate. To
make large dots, dip the
eraser of a pencil into the
paint and dot onto the
ornament. If desired,
sprinkle with glitter. To
make small dots, use the
end of a toothpick or the
handle of a paintbrush.
Let dry.
4 Glue sequin string
around the ornament
top. Let the glue dry. Use
a 10-inch piece of ribbon
to make the permanent
hanger. Tie into a bow or
knot as desired.

jack-o'-lantern ornament

supplies
Round white or orange
glass ornament
Pencil; newspapers
Thick white crafts glue
Glitter in black or pink
1/8- to 1/4-inch-wide
ribbon

what to do
1 Gently draw a
pumpkin face on the
ornament using pencil.
Press lightly to avoid
breaking the ornament.
2 Cover work surface
with newspapers.
Draw on facial features
using glue. While wet,
sprinkle on glitter. Let dry.
3 Tie a ribbon bow at
the top.

starry night ornament

supplies
Round orange glass
ornament
Drinking glass; round
and star-shape clear
and orange gems
Thick white crafts glue
Black and gold cording

what to do
1 Set the ornament in
the glass while
working on one side.
2 Glue gems to the
ornament as desired.
Let dry. Turn the
ornament over. Glue gems
to the remaining side. Let
the glue dry.
3 Wrap and glue cord
around the top. Let
dry. Make a cord hanger.

spider-'n'-web ornament

supplies
Round orange glass
ornament; 1/4-inch-wide
rubber bands
Newspapers
Black spray paint
5 inches of orange
sequins on a string
Thick white crafts glue
Spider ring
1/8-inch-wide satin ribbon

what to do

1 Place a rubber band around the center of the ornament. Place a second band over the topper and around the bottom (the bands will cross in the center). Place two rubber bands between those already on the ornament, making sure all intersect in the same place.

2 In a well-ventilated area, cover work surface with newspapers. Spray-paint a light coat over the ornament. Let dry. Remove the bands.

3 Glue the sequin string around the top. Let dry. Attach a spider ring and ribbon hanger.

halloween swirl ornament

supplies

Round clear glass ornament with removable topper
Newspapers
Acrylic paints in black, yellow, and orange
Thick white crafts glue
2-inch piece of rhinestone trim
1-inch-wide metallic ribbon

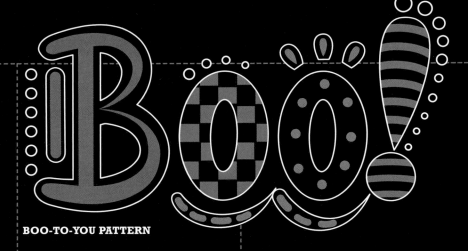

BOO-TO-YOU PATTERN

what to do

1 Remove the topper from the ornament. Set the topper aside.

2 Cover work surface with newspapers. Put small amounts of black, orange, and yellow paints into the ornament. Rotate the ornament so the paints swirl together until the entire inside is covered with paint. Leave the topper off and let dry.

3 Place the topper on the ornament. Glue the rhinestone trim around the ornament top, trimming to fit. Let the glue dry. Thread the ribbon through the ornament top for a hanger.

boo-to-you ornament

supplies

Round white glass ornament
Glass paints in black, purple, and orange
Paintbrush

Needlenose pliers
12-inch-long piece of lead-free solder
Clear silicone glue
Ribbon, if desired

what to do

1 Gently wash and dry the glass ornament. Avoid touching the areas on the ornament to be painted.

2 Looking at the pattern, *above*, as a guide, paint BOO! in black. Let the paint dry.

3 Accent with color as shown, leaving a black border. Let the paint dry.

4 Use needlenose pliers to curl the ends of the solder. Form one end over the B on the ornament and carefully wrap the ornament top with the solder. Glue the solder in place. Let the glue dry. To hang, use the top solder loop or attach a ribbon.

147

velcoming wreath

Set a magical mood by making this quick and inexpensive wreath to welcome all the little folks on Beggars' Night. All it takes are white pony beads sprinkled between twists of colored pipe cleaners to add Halloween sparkle to a grapevine wreath coated in glossy black paint.

supplies
Newspapers
24-inch grapevine wreath
Glossy black spray paint
Pipe cleaners in orange, silver, and black
Round pencil
Scissors
White pony beads
1 yard of 2-inch-wide silver wire-edge ribbon

what to do

1 In a well-ventilated area, cover the work surface with newspapers. Lay the grapevine wreath on the newspapers and spray-paint one side of the wreath using black paint. Let the paint dry. Turn the wreath over and spray-paint the back side. Let the paint dry.

2 Shape several orange and silver pipe cleaners into coils or S-shapes as shown in the photograph, *opposite.* Arrange the coils and S-shapes on the wreath and secure by wrapping one end of each pipe cleaner around a vine on the wreath.

3 To make each long spiral, wrap an orange pipe cleaner around a pencil. Remove the spiral from the pencil and tuck it into the wreath where desired, securing under the vines. Make six or seven spirals and attach them to the wreath.

4 Cut several 2-inch pieces from black pipe cleaners. Thread a white pony bead on each piece. Twist each beaded pipe cleaner piece around the wreath. Continue threading beads between the pipe cleaner shapes until the desired look is achieved.

5 To place the bow on the wreath, slip the piece of ribbon under some of the vines. Tie the ribbon into a bow. Trim the ribbon ends.

roly-poly pumpkin trio

supplies
Pencil; tracing paper
Scissors; compass; ruler
Two 7-inch squares of
green and black plaid
fabric

7-inch square of paper
back fusible web
¼ yard of orange and
black check fabric
2-inch-diameter wood
knob with flat side

Two 1½-inch-diameter
wood knobs, each with
one flat side
Acrylic paints in orange
and black
Paintbrush

These jesterlike
characters bring lots of
giggles as they teeter
with the slightest touch.
Their pipe cleaner arms
bend into all sorts of
funny poses.

Heavy black thread
Sewing needle
Polyester fiberfill
Hot-glue gun and
  glue sticks
3 pipe cleaners
Liquid seam sealant
3½-inch-long straw
  broom
5 yards of 30-gauge
  florist's wire; T-pin

what to do

1 Trace the leaf patterns, *right,* onto tracing paper. Cut out. For small body pattern, use a compass to draw a circle 6¾ inches across onto tracing paper. Cut out. For the large body pattern, draw a circle 8¼ inches across onto tracing paper and cut out.

2 To make leaves, fuse the green and black fabric squares together using fusible web.

3 From orange and black fabric, use patterns to cut one large body, two small bodies, one 1⅛×12½-inch strip, and two 1⅛×10½-inch strips for arms. From fused fabric, cut 5 large and 10 small leaves.

4 Paint the knobs orange. Let dry. With flat sides down, paint faces on the knobs, using the patterns, *right,* as a guide. Let dry.

5 For each body, use a double strand of heavy thread to sew a running stitch ¼ inch from edge of fabric. Stuff with fiberfill. Pull threads and knot.

6 For leaves, make a tuck in rounded end and hot-glue to neck. Hot-glue heads to bodies.

7 For arms, cut pipe cleaners into one 10-inch-long and two 8-inch-long pieces. Apply liquid seam sealant to short ends of orange and black fabric strips. Let dry. Press under ¼ inch on one long side of each fabric strip. Tie a knot ½ inch from one end of each fabric strip. Push one end of long pipe cleaner up against the knot of the long fabric strip. Wrap fabric around pipe cleaner with pressed edge covering raw edge. Slip-stitch closed. Tie a knot in the remaining end of the fabric strip ½ inch from the end, working the knot down against the end of the pipe cleaner. Repeat, using the shorter fabric strips and pipe cleaners.

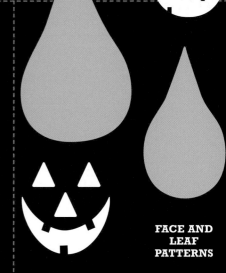

FACE AND LEAF PATTERNS

8 To attach arms, center the longer arm behind the head and underneath the leaves of the larger body. Shape arms to fit curve of head. Glue in place. Attach the arms to the small figures in the same manner.

9 Glue the broom to a character. Let dry.

10 For tendrils, cut florist's wire into twelve 15-inch-long pieces. To curl the wire, wrap each piece around a pencil. Slip off pencil. Apply glue to one end of a tendril and slip it between the leaves, pressing the end into the body. Glue three tendrils around each head. Use a T-pin to make a small hole about ¼ inch deep in the top of each head. Glue one tendril to the top of each head.

wiggling witch

supplies

Two 6×½-inch wood
  dowels
Acrylic paints in
  black, orange,
  and purple
Paintbrush

2 wood hearts
  approximately
  2×1×³⁄₁₆ inches
Hot-glue gun and
  glue sticks
1×½-inch wood dowel
Small wood base
Paint pens in black,
  green, orange, and
  glitter gold
Heavy-duty scissors
4-inch plastic funnel
Black spray paint
Tracing paper
Pencil; scissors
Sheet of white card
  stock
Permanent marking
  pens in black and
  green
Red colored pencil
Thick white crafts glue
Scrap of yellow paper

Crank up "The
Monster Mash"
and give this gal a
tap! With a funnel
for a body, this
happy-go-lucky
witch will bop to
the beat.

what to do

1. **[For legs]**, paint orange and purple stripes on the 6-inch-long dowels. Paint the hearts black for shoes. Let the paint dry.

2. Hot-glue the bottom of each dowel to the center back of one heart. The pointed portion of the heart becomes the toe of the shoe. Hot-glue the legs together by gluing the 1×½-inch wood dowel spacer between the top of each leg. Hot-glue the shoes to the wood base. Use glitter gold to squeeze three gold buttons down the center of each shoe.

3. With heavy-duty scissors, cut the handle from the funnel if necessary. Spray-paint the funnel black and set aside to dry.

4. Trace the patterns, *above right,* onto tracing paper and cut out. Cut the front (with chin) and the back (without chin) head pieces from card stock. Color the hat black using marking pen. Use green to color the hair as shown, *above right,* for front. For back, color entire head area with green. Draw in face

HAT STAR PATTERN

COAT STAR PATTERN

FRONT/BACK HEAD AND HAT PATTERN

SLEEVE AND HAND PATTERN

details using black. Color the mouth and cheeks with red pencil. Outline the hat with black paint pen. Draw a gold hatband. Highlight hair with strokes of green and gold.

5. Cut a length of card stock to go around the neck of the funnel. Color it with black marking pen. Glue strip around neck of funnel. Glue head front to one side of tube and head back to the opposite side.

6. Cut arms from card stock. Color the sleeves black with orange

paint-pen stripes on each cuff area. Outline the stripes with black paint pen. Let the paint dry.

7. Use crafts glue to glue the arms to the sides of the body. Draw buttons down the front of the coat using glitter gold paint pen.

8. Cut stars from yellow paper and glue the large one to coat and the small one to the tip of each hat side.

jack-o'-witchy

Any type of jack-o'-lantern, carved or made of foam, takes on a bewitching personality when topped with this starstruck hat. The purchased hat is dotted with purple and orange glitter. Placed on a handful of sparkling shred, this clever creation makes a stunning centerpiece. For extra shrieks, place a plastic lizard or frog on the brim.

supplies
Tracing paper
Pencil
Scissors
White pencil
Witch hat
Lime green paint pen
Thick white crafts glue
Paintbrush
Glitter in purple and
  orange
Foam or carved
  jack-o'-lantern
Sparkling shred, such
  as Mylar
Plastic lizard
  or frog

what to do
1 Trace star patterns, *below,* and cut out. Use white pencil to trace around star shapes on witch hat.

2 Use a lime green paint pen to outline star shapes. Let the paint pen dry.

3 Paint a thin coat of crafts glue inside each star shape. While the glue is wet, sprinkle it with glitter. Let it dry. Shake off excess glitter.

4 Place jack-o'-lantern on a handful of shred. Arrange the hat on the jack-o'-lantern, and a plastic lizard or frog on the brim.

SMALL STAR
PATTERN

LARGE STAR
PATTERN

155

ghoulish garlands

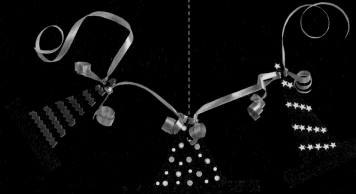

Whatever the theme of your Halloween decorating, design a garland that fits right into the plan. From funky witch hats to gem-covered masks and dancing candy corn with pony bead spacers—these festive trims give holiday pizzazz to doors, mantels, windows, banisters, and more!

supplies
Tracing paper; pencil
Scissors; white pencil
Craft foam in orange, yellow, white, purple, green, and black
Round and star-shape paper punches
Pinking shears
Thick white crafts glue

Gems
Permanent silver marking pen
Plastic-coated wires in desired colors
Pipe cleaners
Curling ribbon
Pony beads; ice pick

what to do

1 Trace the garland patterns from *pages 158–159* onto tracing paper. Cut out the shapes.

2 Trace around patterns as many times as desired on craft foam. If pencil lines do not show up, use a white pencil. Cut out the shapes.

3 To make tiny circle or star shapes, punch out with a paper punch. To make zigzag stripes, cut with pinking shears.

4 Layer and glue pieces together, using the patterns as a guide. Let the glue dry.

5 Embellish the foam pieces with gems, small snippets of foam, or silver marking pen details.

6 To connect the garland pieces, use the photographs, *opposite* and *above,* for ideas. Use a paper punch to make holes if needed. Thread wire, pipe cleaners, or curling ribbon through the holes, threading beads if desired. To form wire into a spiral, wrap it around an ice pick before connecting it to foam shapes.

continued on page 158

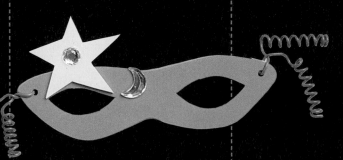

157

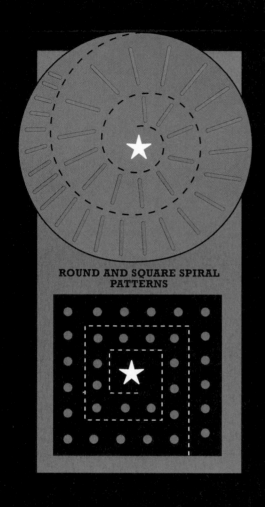

ROUND AND SQUARE SPIRAL PATTERNS

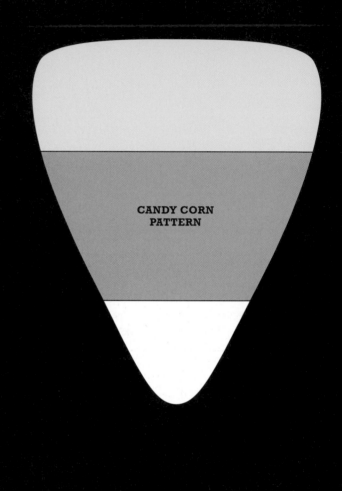

CANDY CORN PATTERN

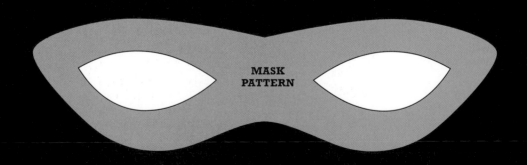

MASK PATTERN

BOO!

BOO LETTERING PATTERN

**SQUATTY WITCH HAT
PATTERN**

**TALL WITCH HAT
PATTERN**

159

hallow's eve wind sock

When the chilly October winds blow, let this colorful trim catch each gust. The Halloween wind sock is stitched using several colors of yarn and simple stitches that work quickly over seven-count plastic canvas. The nylon streamers are edged with sequins on a string that sparkle day or night.

supplies

Red Heart Super Saver worsted weight yarn in kiwi (651), bright yellow (324), black (312), lavender (358), white (311), and vibrant orange (354)
No. 13 tapestry needle
7-count plastic canvas, cut 85 holes × 35 holes
Cotton embroidery floss in black and white
Scissors; yardstick
Hot-glue gun and glue sticks
1 yard of black nylon fabric
Cutting mat
Rotary cutter

Approximately 20 yards of orange and black sequins on a string

what to do

1 Following the chart on *page 163,* stitch the design on plastic canvas using the continental stitch. Start in the fifth hole at the top left, beginning with the fifth stitch. Do not stitch the first four columns of the left edge of the design. Stitch all French knots using four strands of floss.

2 After stitching is completed, except for the four left columns, fold the plastic canvas to form a tube. Overlap the four columns of holes on each end and finish stitching the design, going through both layers of canvas to join the ends.

continued on page 162

3 Overcast the top and the bottom edges using black yarn.

4 Cut two 30-inch lengths each from orange, kiwi, and black yarns. Tie the yarns together on one end and divide the yarns into the two yarns of each color. Braid together for 17 inches. Tie the yarns together at the end of the braid and trim any excess yarn. Glue one end inside the top of the plastic canvas tube and glue the other end on the opposite side to form a hanger.

5 Spread nylon fabric on the cutting mat. Use a rotary cutter to cut the fabric into 10 lengthwise strips that are 2 inches wide as shown on the cutting diagram, *right.* Stop cutting 1 inch from the top edge. Apply glue along the long cut edges and press sequins into glue along edge. Let the glue dry. Apply glue along the bottom inside edge of the plastic canvas tube $\frac{1}{2}$ inch from the bottom. Glue the top edge of the nylon streamers to the tube.

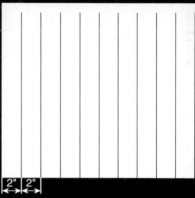

NYLON FABRIC-CUTTING DIAGRAM

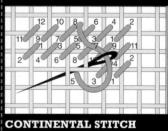

CONTINENTAL STITCH

FRENCH KNOT

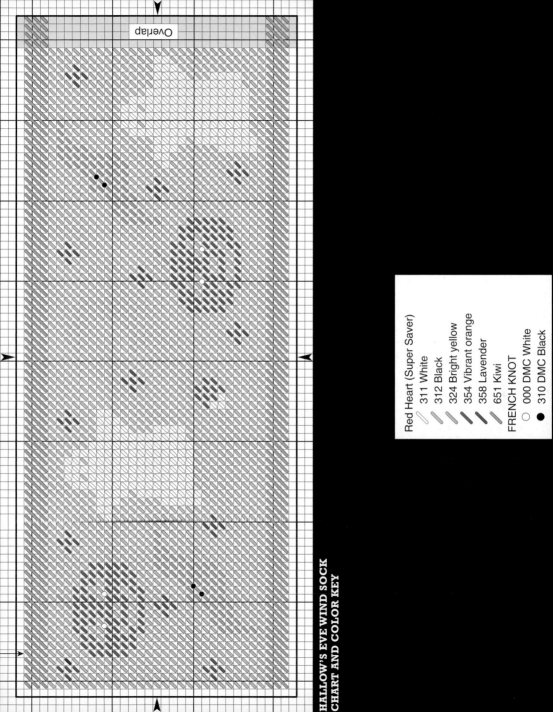

Overlap

HALLOW'S EVE WIND SOCK
CHART AND COLOR KEY

Red Heart (Super Saver)

⟋ 311 White
⟋ 312 Black
⟋ 324 Bright yellow
⟋ 354 Vibrant orange
⟋ 358 Lavender
⟋ 651 Kiwi

FRENCH KNOT

○ 000 DMC White
● 310 DMC Black

candy corn baskets

Black wire baskets transform into Halloween accents when trimmed with a band of clay candy corn. Use the decorations as candleholders or as candy dishes to keep treats on hand for little tricksters.

supplies
Polymer clay, such as
  Sculpey, in white,
  yellow, and orange
Crafts knife
Black wire basket
  or bowl

what to do

1 Work the clay in your hands to make it warm and pliable. Roll each color of clay into a long rope. The white clay should be approximately 1/2 inch wide and the yellow and orange clay slightly thinner.

2 Gently flatten both the white and the yellow ropes by pressing your finger down the length of each rope.

3 Place the yellow rope over the white, joining them with slight pressure. Pinch the top of the orange rope to make it triangular and then press the bottom side on top of the yellow rope.

4 Cut 1/4-inch slices off the finished roll. Each slice will need to be smoothed and finished to look like candy corn by pinching the outside edges with your fingertips. Firmly press the white bottom of the finished candy corn onto the rim of the container. Bake the clay-topped container according to the clay manufacturer's directions. Use caution with the finished piece. Although the clay is hardened, it can chip.

165

haunting centerpiece

It's eerie! It's scary! It's the perfect centerpiece for Halloween! Some spray paint and ghoulish glitter leave their fiendish marks on these flea market finds. Arrange the items on an ornate silver tray and spook the masks off everyone at your next gruesome gala.

supplies

Old vases, candleholders, ornate trays and picture frames, metal bowls with handles, pieces of chain, etc.
Newspapers
Spray paint in black and pewter
Plastic canvas and scissors, if needed
Decoupage medium
Paintbrush
Glitter in black and silver
Silver candles
Artificial spiderweb
Dry ice

what to do

1 In a well-ventilated work area, place items to be painted on newspapers. Spray-paint the items black. If painting a frame such as the oval one, *opposite,* first remove the glass. Paint one side of the glass. Let dry. Spray the items with pewter paint, allowing some of the black to show through. Let dry. Reassemble the frame. A pattern shows through the glass of this frame because of the plastic backing piece. If your frame does not have this type of backing, cut and insert a piece of plastic canvas to achieve the effect.

2 Brush decoupage medium on the areas where glitter is desired. Sprinkle glitters onto the wet decoupage medium. Let dry. Shake off excess.

3 Arrange items on tray, situating candles, spiderweb, and dry ice as desired.

Caution: *Dry ice can cause severe burns. Always wear gloves when handling dry ice.*

FISHBOWL
FLOWERPOT

FISHY FISHBOWL

fiendish fish- bowls

Whether you like to decoupage, paint, or decorate, these clever fishbowls are so easy to make, you can whip up one before a ghost can say boo! Use them to hold Halloween candy or an unexpected treat, such as goldfish or a seasonal plant. Turn the page for the instructions.

BEWARE TREAT HOLDER

fishbowl flowerpot

supplies

8-inch-high round fishbowl
Crepe paper streamers in orange, yellow, and black
Pinking shears
Glossy decoupage medium; paintbrush
Black glass paint
Pencil with round eraser
3 black pipe cleaners
Pony beads in black, yellow, and orange
Potted plant

what to do

1 Wash and dry the fishbowl. Cut one-third of each roll of streamers into squares and strips using pinking shears.

2 Working on small sections at a time, brush decoupage medium on the inside of the fishbowl. Press crepe paper pieces onto decoupage medium and smooth out with a paintbrush. Change colors and overlap pieces as desired. When the entire inside of the fishbowl is covered with crepe paper pieces, apply a coat of decoupage medium over the entire inside surface. Let dry.

3 To make black polka dots on the outside of the fishbowl, dip the eraser of a pencil into paint and dot onto the surface. Let dry.

4 Twist the ends of the pipe cleaners together to form a longer piece. Thread a black pony bead on one end and twist the pipe cleaner to secure it. Continue threading pony beads, alternating the orange and yellow with black. Secure a black bead on the end. Wrap the beaded piece around the top of the fishbowl and twist to secure.

5 Set a potted plant in the fishbowl flowerpot.

fishy fishbowl

supplies

6-inch-high fishbowl
Glass paint in orange and black
Pencil with round eraser
Pipe cleaners in black, orange, purple, and lime green
2 jack-o'-lantern jingle bells

what to do

1 Wash and dry the fishbowl. Avoid touching the areas to be painted. For polka dots, dip the eraser of the pencil into paint and dot onto the surface. Wash off the eraser before changing colors. Let the paint dry. Bake the painted piece in the oven if instructed by the paint manufacturer.

2 To make the pipe cleaner "beads," wrap each pipe cleaner tightly around a pencil. Remove pencil. You will need approximately 13 black beads and 4 of each other color.

3 Twist three black pipe cleaners together to make a longer piece. Insert one end through the loop of a jingle bell. Twist to secure. Beginning with a black pipe cleaner bead, thread beads onto the straight pipe cleaner piece, alternating the colors with black. End with black and attach the remaining jingle bell.

4 Wrap the beaded length around the top of the fishbowl. Twist to secure, leaving six beads on each tail. Twist tails to form a bow as shown in the photo, *opposite.*

beware treat holder

supplies
Fishbowl
Black vinyl adhesive lettering
Thick white crafts glue
Plastic spiders in orange and black
Artificial spiderweb
Rubber band
Scissors

24-inch-long piece of ¼-inch-wide orange ribbon

what to do
1 Wash and dry the fishbowl.

2 Using small adhesive letters, spell out TAKE ONE IF YOU DARE across the top front of the fishbowl, curving as necessary. Spell BOO! at the bottom front. Use large letters to spell BEWARE across the center of the fishbowl front.

3 Glue a spider inside the fishbowl next to the word BOO. Let dry.

4 Wrap a small piece of web around the fishbowl. Place a rubber band around the rim to hold web in place. Trim excess from the top. Tie a ribbon around the rim. Place spiders in the web.

171

Like dew on a real web, these beaded versions glisten in the sunlight. Make them in black or white; then perch the wire web spinners close by.

spiderweb

supplies
Wire cutters
Yardstick
20-gauge white or
  black wire
6-mm black faceted or
  pearl beads
Pliers
24-gauge silver wire
Monofilament thread

what to do
1 Cut four lengths of 20-gauge wire 2 to 3 feet long for a larger web or 1 to 1½ feet long for a smaller web. Cut a 2½-inch length of wire and wrap it three times around the center of all four wires to secure. Twist the short wire ends together and then trim off any excess.

2 Spread out the wires to become the spokes of the web. Work with one spoke at a time and thread the entire length with beads. Turn over the wire end with pliers. The loop will prevent the beads from falling off. Continue until the remaining spokes are completed.

3 Cut a 2-foot length (reduce the length if making the smaller web) of 24-gauge wire. Twist the end around one of the beaded spokes 1½ inches out from the center of the web. Thread seven to nine beads onto the wire and then wrap it around the next spoke. Continue threading beads and wrapping the wire around each spoke to encircle the web. Twist the wire end and trim remaining wire.

4 Cut a 3-foot length of 24-gauge wire for the next circle of the web. Work around the web again, increasing the number of beads to fill the space between spokes. Cut a longer wire and increase the number of beads for the third time around the web. Hang the web from thread.

spider

supplies
Wire cutters; ruler
18-gauge yellow craft
  wire; pliers
2 black faceted or
  pearl beads
24-gauge wire

what to do
1 Cut five 5-inch lengths of wire. Group four of the wires together. Tightly wrap one end of the fifth wire around the center of the group four times. Spiral the end of the fifth wire to make the body.

2 Separate the spider's legs and loop over each end to make its feet. Thread two bead eyes on a 2-inch length of

24-gauge wire. Position the beads over the top of the wrapped wire body. Bring the wire ends down between the first and second legs on both sides. Twist the ends together under the body and trim away any excess wire.

Light the path to your haunted mansion with these solemn milk jug luminarias. For little investment, make enough characters to line your drive on Halloween night.

supplies

- Gallon plastic jugs, rinsed and labels removed
- Utility knife
- Tracing paper
- Pencil
- Scissors
- Tape
- Paint marking pens in silver, orange, green, yellow, red, and black
- Goo Gone
- Paper towels and cotton swabs
- Monster: 2 each of bolts, nuts, washers, and white and black craft foam scraps, such as Fun Foam
- Cat: two 12-inch lengths of 20-gauge steel wire and black craft foam
- Thick white crafts glue
- Darning needle and pliers
- Sand, candles, and matches, a flashlight, or a string of lights

what to do

1 Carefully cut the spout and handle off each jug. Enlarge and trace the patterns, *pages 176–177.* Cut out face patterns and tape to the inside of jugs.

2 Outline the skull with silver, the monster head with green, and the cat with black. To spread the color over the face of the jug, squeeze a few drops of Goo Gone onto a folded paper towel and rub it over the marking pen on the jug. Continue working around the edges, wiping the paint toward the center of your design. For the skull, draw an additional line of orange around the skull and spread it outward with the paper towel and Goo Gone. Let dry.

3 After the paint has dried, draw eyes, nose, teeth, hair, and scar with the paint pens. Remove any mistakes or unwanted marks by squeezing Goo Gone onto the end of a cotton swab and then wiping away the problem spot (use paper towel for larger areas). Once you're pleased with your design, outline the features with the black paint pen.

4 To insert the bolts in the monster's neck, poke a hole on each side of his neck with scissors. Thread a washer onto the bolt and push it through the hole. Reaching inside the jug, screw a nut onto the end of the bolt. Use the cat ear, collar, and bow tie patterns to cut pieces from foam. Slip the collar under the washers and glue the bow tie to the center of the collar. Glue the cat ears in place.

5 To thread the whiskers onto the cat, poke two holes on each side of the nose with a needle. Poke the wire into a hole on one side of the nose and out the hole on the other side. Repeat the process with the second wire. Use pliers to make curls on wire ends.

6 Place a flashlight or string of lights in the jug. Or, if using candles, pour 2 to 3 inches of sand in the bottom of each jug. Place a candle in the center. Never leave burning candles unattended.

continued on page 176

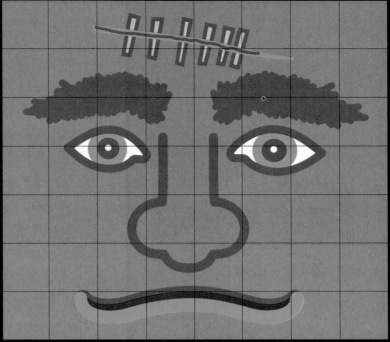

MONSTER LUMINARIA PATTERN   **1 SQUARE = 1 INCH**

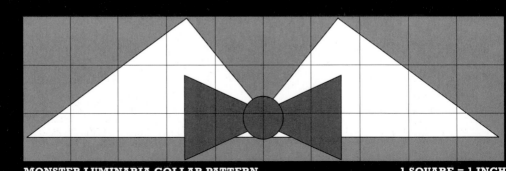

MONSTER LUMINARIA COLLAR PATTERN   **1 SQUARE = 1 INCH**

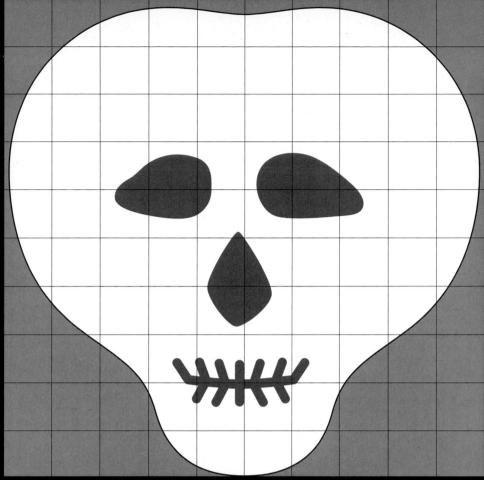

SKULL LUMINARIA PATTERN　　　　　　　　　　　　**1 SQUARE = 1 INCH**

CAT LUMINARIA PATTERN　　　　　　　　　　　　**1 SQUARE = 1 INCH**

pumpkin wreath

Welcome Halloween visitors with a cheerful wreath of animated pumpkins. Use our wreath for inspiration, but have fun making your own funny faces from lightweight clay. Drape the wreath with artificial spiderwebbing to complete the look.

supplies

10-inch wreath form of wire or foam, such as Styrofoam
Wide masking tape
Air-dry clay, such as Crayola Model Magic
Rolling pin; ruler
2- to 3½-inch round biscuit or cookie cutters
Sharp knife
Thick white crafts glue
Toothpick
Acrylic paints in orange, yellow, black, lime green, and green
Paintbrush
Strong adhesive, such as E6000
Black curling ribbon
Scissors
Artificial spiderweb

what to do

1 Using masking tape, wrap the wreath form until covered. Set aside.

2 To make pumpkins, roll out clay about ⅛ inch thick. Cut circles with various sizes of the round cutters. Work quickly as the clay dries fast and keep extra clay tightly wrapped.

3 Distort the circles slightly by pulling into oblong shapes as desired. Use a knife to press curved lines into the pumpkins.

4 Form clay eyes, noses, and mouths. Cut rectangles for stems. Position the pieces on the pumpkins. Use a toothpick to spread a dab of crafts glue to attach them. Cut simple leaf shapes. Use the knife to draw leaf veins. Let the clay pieces dry.

5 Paint the pumpkins orange, the stems green, the leaves both shades of green, and the facial features yellow and black. Let dry.

6 Generously apply adhesive to pumpkin backs and leaves. Attach to wreath form using the photo, *opposite,* as a guide. Let dry.

7 To curl pieces of ribbon, hold scissors at an angle against ribbon, pulling ribbon taut against blade. Glue ribbons between the clay pieces. Let dry. Stretch web as desired.

Pieces of wire appear to lace the miniature pumpkins together as they encircle a towering candle. Dripping with white wax and orange and black glitter, the three-wick candle is an appealing addition to this Halloween centerpiece.

supplies

White wax, candle, or paraffin
Old metal saucepan and metal can
3-wick black candle
Orange and black glitter
Ruler
18-gauge wire
Wire cutters
Soup can
Pliers
Awl
Small round tray
Approximately 10 miniature pumpkins

what to do

1 To melt wax, break up pieces and place in metal can. Place can in a saucepan filled halfway with water. Heat on stove until melted, watching wax constantly. Pour the wax over top and edges of the black candle. Sprinkle glitter over the wet wax.

2 Cut ten 6-inch-long and ten 3-inch-long pieces of wire. If using more pumpkins, cut more wires as needed.

3 Bend the long pieces of wire around a soup can to shape into an arch. Use pliers to shape the short pieces of wire into Vs.

4 With an awl, poke holes into the top and sides of each pumpkin as shown in the photo, *opposite.*

5 Arrange the candle and pumpkins on a tray. Insert the wires into the pumpkins as shown. Never leave burning candles unattended.

shrieking shakers

Although these shakers are quiet as a mummy, they just might elicit some shrieks from you! Pick a favorite Halloween toy to place inside your one-of-a-kind shaker to make it as scary or as silly as you like. These suspenseful toys make great party favors for special ghouls and boys.

supplies

Small plastic Halloween toys such as spiders, pumpkins, skeletons, mummies, witches, etc.
Pencil
Glass jar and lid
Plastic yogurt or margarine container lid
Scissors
Hot-glue gun and glue sticks
Thumbtacks
Glycerin
Glitter, sequins, and confetti
Food coloring in green, yellow, and blue
Paper towel
Feather boa

what to do

1 Select a toy to place inside the jar. Trace the top of the jar lid onto a plastic lid and cut out the circle. Anchor the base of the toy to the plastic circle by first hot-gluing it and then pushing thumbtacks up through the underside of the circle and into the base of the toy. Glue the plastic lid inside the jar lid.

2 Fill the jar halfway with water and the remainder with glycerin, allowing enough space to accommodate the toy. Sprinkle glitter, sequins, and confetti in any combination into the filled jar. To color the shaker mixture green, place a half drop each of green and yellow food coloring into the shaker mixture. To make the water blue, add a half drop of blue.

3 Screw the jar lid tightly in place. Invert jar onto a paper towel to test for leaks. Hot-glue around the edge of the lid and wrap the feather boa around the glue. Trim away excess. Glue a plastic spider to the top of the jar if desired.

pumpkinland royalty

Coronate a new corn queen and king to reign over your Halloween traditions.

supplies

Newspapers
White spray primer
5×7- and 6½×9-inch beveled wood pieces
Acrylic paints in black, yellow, orange, lime green, purple, grass green, and magenta
Medium flat and fine liner paintbrushes
Thick white crafts glue
2 ears of colored corn
1 gallon water
¼ cup bleach
Scissors; knife
Drill and small drill bit
Two 3-inch screws
Hot-glue gun and glue sticks
Foxtail grass or similar dried flowers
Assorted gems
Tracing paper and soft lead pencil
2 miniature pumpkins, real or artificial
Black permanent marking pen
Candy corn
Metallic gold spray paint
Black braid trim

what to do

1 In a well-ventilated work area, cover work surface with newspapers. Spray one side of each wood piece and the edges with white primer. Let the paint dry. Turn the wood pieces over and apply spray primer.

2 Paint the top surfaces of the wood pieces black. Using the photograph, *opposite,* for inspiration, paint orange and purple borders, yellow dots, magenta stripes, and lime green wavy lines. To paint dots, dip the handle of a paintbrush into paint and dot onto surface.

3 Glue the smaller wood piece in the center of the larger piece. Let the glue dry.

4 To prepare the ears of corn, carefully remove husks, keeping them intact. To soften and clean the husks, mix ¼ cup bleach and 1 gallon water. Soak the husks in the bleach water 10 minutes. Separate each piece so it is easier to work with. Dab off excess water.

5 Trim the damp, pliable husks to the desired lengths. Trim the outer husks shorter than the inner husks. Paint the husks using purple, magenta, lime green, and grass green. Paint stems of the pumpkins green. Shape the husks back into their original shape and let dry. Cut the ends of each ear of corn so they are flat.

6 Drill two holes in the bottom of the wood base for the ears of corn to stand. Insert screws into the wood base and screw on the ears of corn.

7 Reattach layers of painted husks to the ears of corn using hot glue. Decorate with foxtail grass or dried flowers and gems.

continued on page 186

8 Trace the face patterns, *right,* or make your own on tracing paper. Color the back of each tracing paper with a soft lead pencil. Place the patterns on the pumpkins and trace the pattern lines to transfer the drawings. Darken the pencil lines by drawing over them with a black marking pen.

9 Hot-glue the pumpkin heads on top of the corn.

10 In a well-ventilated work area, cover the work surface with newspapers. Spray the candy corn with gold spray paint. Let dry. Hot-glue the candy corn onto the pumpkin heads in a crown shape. Hot-glue gems to the crown tips. Glue black braid trim around the base of each crown.

KING'S FACE PATTERN

QUEEN'S FACE PATTERN

pumpkins in a row

Nestled in chunky lavender bath salts, these pumpkins make enticing candleholders. Change the bath salts and taper candles to seasonal colors, and this arrangement can be enjoyed all year long.

supplies
Miniature pumpkins
Sharp knife
Taper candles
Lavender bath salts
Shallow container, such as a planter or serving dish
Matches

what to do
1 Cut a hole in the top of each pumpkin just large enough to fit a taper candle.

2 Fill the container two-thirds of the way with bath salts. Arrange the pumpkins in the salt, pushing down gently to secure.

3 Place a candle in each pumpkin. Sprinkle a pinch of bath salt around the base of each candle. Never leave burning candles unattended.

rustic candelabra

supplies
Rake
Sharp knife
Miniature pumpkins
Votive candles
Metal skewer or ice pick
18-gauge wire
Wire cutters
Matches

what to do

1 Secure the rake handle in the ground.

2 Cut the tops off the pumpkins and discard. Cut out areas large enough to accommodate a votive candle.

3 Using a metal skewer or ice pick, punch two or three small holes around the top edge of the pumpkin.

4 Cut two or three equal lengths of 18-gauge wire. Thread one through each hole, twisting to secure. Bring the loose ends of wire together and loop around the rake tines. Twist to secure. Insert a candle in each pumpkin. Never leave burning candles unattended.

Fashion an outdoor pumpkin candelabra from an antique wood garden rake. Suspend the pumpkins in place with wire hangers.

Greet guests with a wreath that sets the stage for Halloween fun.

pumpkin ring wreath

supplies

**Drill and ⁹⁄₆₄-inch
  drill bit**
Miniature pumpkins
**20-gauge aluminum
  wire**
Wire cutters
**Wire wreath form
  (available at crafts and
  floral supply stores)**
Dry moss
2-inch-wide ribbon
Scissors

what to do

1 Drill a hole horizontally through each miniature pumpkin, positioning the holes toward the bottom of the pumpkin where they won't be very visible.

2 String a piece of wire through the openings in one pumpkin. Place pumpkin on a wire wreath form, wires perpendicular to the form. Bring wires around to the back of the form and twist them to secure to the form.

Continue wiring pumpkins to the form until it is covered. Fill the spaces between the pumpkins with dry moss by wiring it to the form.

3 Tie a generous bow from ribbon. Wire to the top of the wreath. Trim the ribbon ends.

witchy welcome sign

Hanging from a witch's broom, these words of warning are perfect for the entrance of any haunted house.

supplies
Broom with wood handle
Medium-grit sandpaper
Tack cloth; newspapers
Spray paints in silver
  and purple
Pencil; ruler
Acrylic enamel paints in
  black and orange
$1/2$- and 1-inch flat
  paintbrushes
Tracing paper; scissors
2×4-foot piece of plywood
Band saw
Acrylic paints in white,
  black, bright green,
  purple, and bright
  orange
Crackle medium
Transfer paper
Drill and $1/16$-inch bit
6 small eye screws
6 feet of chain

what to do

1 Sand broom handle and wipe with tack cloth. In a well-ventilated work area, cover work surface with newspapers. Spray-paint the broom bristles silver. Shade as desired with purple. Let dry.

2 Use a pencil and ruler to mark broom handle in 2-inch increments. Paint alternating black and orange stripes around broom handle using the marks as guides. Let dry.

3 Enlarge and trace the sign pattern and lettering, *below.* Cut out the sign shape. Draw around the sign shape on plywood. Cut out. Sand and wipe edges.

4 Paint the sign using white acrylic. Let dry. Apply a thick coat of crackle medium to the front of the sign. Let dry. Paint over the crackle medium with black acrylic, without overlapping brushstrokes. Let dry.

5 Paint the edges of the sign silver. Let dry.

6 Use transfer paper to transfer the lettering to the sign. Using the pattern as a guide, paint the letters with acrylic paints. Shade edges of the sign with green and orange. Let dry.

7 Drill two $1/16$-inch holes each in the top and bottom of the broom handle and in the top of the sign as shown in the photo, *opposite.* Screw an eye screw into each hole. Attach chain pieces to each of the eye screws.

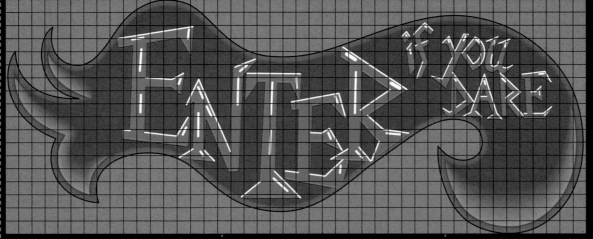

WITCHY WELCOME SIGN PATTERN   1 SQUARE = 1 INCH

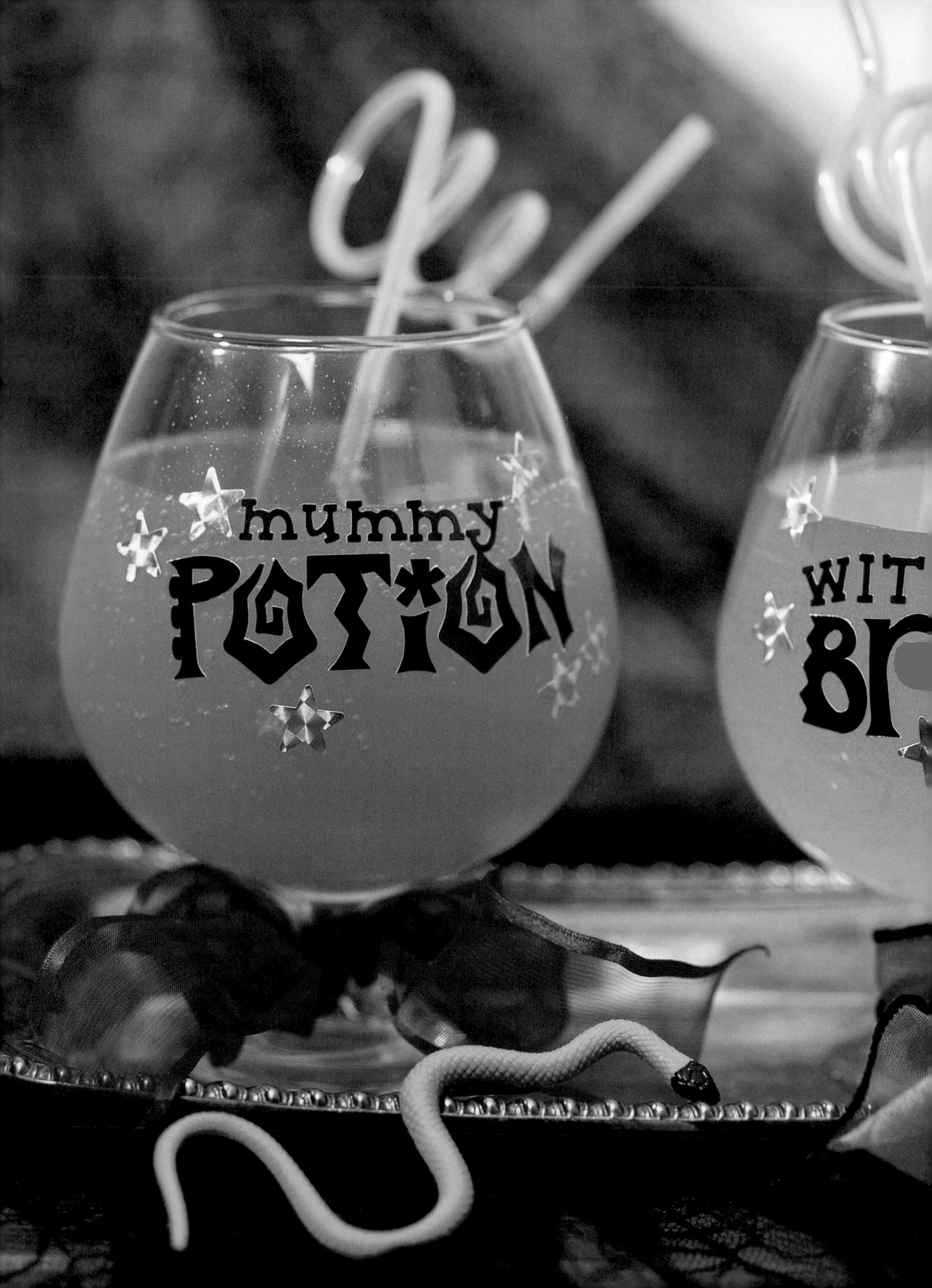
mummy
POT*ON
WIT
BR

goblin goblets

These generous glasses are perfect for a jumbo serving of chilled Halloween potion. The sticker designs go on quick as a bat, so make one for each guest at your gruesome gathering.

supplies

Clear glass goblets
³/₈- and 1-inch black adhesive letters (available in the scrapbooking section of crafts stores)
¹/₂-inch metallic silver star stickers
1- to 1¹/₂-inch-wide wire-edge ribbon
Yardstick; scissors

what to do

1 Wash and dry the goblets. Avoid touching the surface where the stickers will be attached.

2 Decide on letter placement. Starting with large letters, peel and apply to goblet to spell the word BREW or POTION.

3 Center and apply the small letters above the first, spelling the word WITCHES' or MUMMY.

4 Press star stickers randomly around the lettering, keeping away from the rim of the glass.

5 Cut an 18-inch length of ribbon. Tie the ribbon into a bow around the stem of the goblet. Trim the ribbon ends.

Squeeze the wrapped handle to remove any air pockets and to ensure the clay is tightly connected. Smooth away any overlaps or dings with your fingertips. Firmly press doll eyes into the front and back of the clay-covered handle.

3 Bake the decorated tableware according to polymer clay package directions. Let cool. If any of the doll eyes loosen or fall out after baking, glue them back in place and let dry.

4 Carefully hand wash tableware after use. Avoid dropping or banging hardened polymer clay, as it may chip or break.

Start the party off right with a tangled arachnid door decoration.

wired welcome web

supplies

Pruning shears
Forked branch
Acrylic paint in black, silver, or metallic gold
1/2-inch flat paintbrush
Glitter
24-gauge orange, black, or golden wire
Wire cutters; yardstick
Beaded or large plastic spider
Thick white crafts glue
Glitter puff paint, optional

what to do

1 Use pruning shears to trim the branch ends. Paint the branch with the desired color of paint. Sprinkle glitter onto the wet paint and let the branch dry.

2 Cut six or seven 12- to 15-inch lengths of wire. Wrap one end of a wire piece around one side of the forked branch. Position the center of the wire for the middle of the web. Wrap the other end of the wire to the opposite branch. Repeat the process with the remaining wires until all the spokes of the web are positioned.

3 Cut a 16-inch length of wire. Wrap the end of the wire around one of the spokes. Work the other end of the wire around each spoke of the web for a complete spiral. Poke the end of the wire into the spider and glue it in place.

4 If desired, create dewdrops of puff paint on the spiderweb and let dry before hanging.

195

halloween hurricane

Light up your own miniature Halloween sky with this hurricane shade painted with a witch in flight.

supplies

Hurricane shade
Tracing paper; pencil
Scissors; tape
Fine-point permanent
 black pen, such as
 Pigma
Oven-bake glass paints
 in black and yellow
Paintbrushes
Fingernail polish
 remover, toothpick, and
 crafts knife, if needed
Candle; matches

what to do

1 Wash and dry the hurricane shade. Avoid touching the areas to be painted.

2 Trace the patterns, *opposite.* Cut out. Tape patterns onto glass and trace around large shapes with the black pen. The stars and vines will be drawn in later. Remove the patterns. Paint the moon and pumpkin eyes yellow. Paint the remaining designs black. Several coats of paint are necessary. Allow to dry between coats.

3 Use black pen to draw stars and vines. Paint over the lines with black paint. Any visible pen lines can be removed by dipping end of a toothpick into fingernail polish remover and then applying to unwanted lines. Unwanted paint can be removed by scraping with a crafts knife. Bake the hurricane, if necessary, according to the paint manufacturer's directions. Let cool. Never leave burning candles unattended.

HALLOWEEN HURRICANE
WITCH PATTERN

HALLOWEEN HURRICANE
PUMPKIN PATTERNS

197

Make a different goblet base for every guest using assorted colors and designs of Halloween paper.

supplies

Inexpensive clear glass wine goblets
Pencil; scissors
Assorted patterned scrapbook paper in black, white, and orange
Halloween stickers
Outdoor decoupage medium, such as Mod Podge
Paintbrush; waterproof paint marking pens in silver, white, and black, optional

what to do

1 Trace the base of the wine goblet onto the patterned paper. Cut out the circle. Adhere stickers where desired on the paper circles. Remember that stickers in the center of the circle may be obscured by the stem. Check to see if the desired look is achieved by placing the circle under the base of glass. Make any necessary adjustments.

2 Brush a coat of decoupage medium over the top of the decorated circle. Push the circle onto the base of the wine goblet. Be careful to press out any air that may be trapped in the concave center. Apply another coat of decoupage medium over the underside of paper. Let decoupage medium dry. Follow the package instructions to apply three more coats of decoupage medium.

3 For dimension, use the paint pens to draw spots on the glass over the image. Let the paint dry before use. Carefully hand wash the bowl of the wine goblet and wipe the stem and base clean. The base is water-repellent however, avoid submerging it in water.

rat race snack set

Serve up a snack on these silly dishes. Spiders and rats race toward the center, creating quite a conversation piece for a Halloween party.

supplies

Glass snack tray and tumbler (The tray in the photo has raised watermelon seed designs on the bottom. This is a common pattern for snack sets. The tumbler did not come with the set. Pieces like these are often available in flea markets and antiques stores.)

Newspapers or waxed paper

Glass paints in white, black, light orange, orange, and purple

Disposable plate

Toothpick

Small round paintbrush

Pencil with round eraser

what to do

1 Wash and dry the dishes. Avoid touching the areas to be painted.

2 Cover the work surface with newspapers or waxed paper. Turn the tray upside down. The painting is done on the bottom of the tray in reverse order. For the eye pupils, dip the end of a toothpick into black paint. Make two dots, approximately $1/8$ inch apart, on each pointed end of the watermelon seed designs. Let dry.

3 Dip the handle of a small paintbrush into white paint. Center white dots over the black dots as shown in Photo 1, *top right*. Let dry.

4 Paint the seed shapes either black or gray (a mix of black and white) to make the bodies of spiders and rats as shown in Photo 2. Paint eight legs for the spiders and a tail for each rat.

5 Use a toothpick to make three black dots between each rat.

6 For the large dots on the tray and on the glass, dip a pencil eraser into paint and dot onto the surface. Let dry. Embellish with smaller dots using the handle of a paintbrush. Let dry.

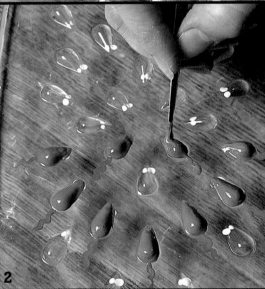

7 If desired, paint the tray handle sections alternating black and purple. Let dry.

8 Bake the glassware in the oven if instructed by the paint manufacturer. Let cool. Follow the paint instructions for washing the dishes.

howls and owls light

Flickering like real flames, this layered design casts a mysterious illusion.

CANDLEHOLDER BACK VIEW

supplies

White glass paint; water
Large glass brandy
  snifter
Paintbrush
Newspapers
Frosted glass spray
  paint in red and yellow
Tracing paper
Pencil
Scissors
Tape
Liquid leading

what to do

1 Thin white glass paint with water to a drippy consistency. Using the pattern on *page 204* as a guide, paint a basic ghost shape on the inside of the glass snifter. Randomly paint wavy vertical lines as shown in Photo 1, *right.* Allow paint to drip and run. Let dry.

2 In a well-ventilated work area, place snifter upside down on newspapers. Spray the rim of snifter red, fading off several inches from the top edge. Spray the heaviest color toward the rim. Spray the base and stem of snifter. Let dry.

3 Spray over the entire outside with an even coat of yellow as shown in Photo 2. Colors will overlap to create a deeper orange and a deep yellow. Let dry.

4 Trace the bat and owl patterns, *page 204,* or draw any freehand Halloween pattern onto paper. Cut out patterns. Tape patterns onto the snifter. Trace around designs. Randomly draw loops and swirls with a pencil. Remove patterns.

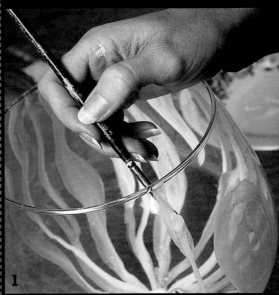

5 Outline the pencil drawing with liquid leading. Use a paintbrush to paint the solid areas. Let dry.

continued on page 204

HOWLS AND OWLS LIGHT PATTERNS

beaded candle cuff

Let the colors of Halloween shine through with glass beads in purple, orange, black, green, and yellow. Dangle the beads from a wire zigzag that hugs the top of a candleholder.

supplies
Brass wire
Wire cutters; ruler
Candle in round glass candleholder
1½-inch-long golden eye pins
Glass beads in purple, orange, black, green, and yellow
Needlenose pliers

what to do
1 Cut a 16-inch length of wire; bend the wire into a strip of zigzags, each about 1 inch high.

2 Align the center of the zigzags with the rim of the candleholder. Fold the wire zigzags over the candleholder edge. Trim excess wire.

3 Place one to three beads on an eye pin. Using needlenose pliers, bend the end of the eye pin. Hook the eye pin onto the wire zigzag. Using the pliers, close the opening in the eye pin to secure. Hang a beaded pin from each wire zigzag loop on the outside of the candleholder. Never leave burning candles unattended.

spooky treats

and holders

ghoulish goodies to concoct

bewitching treat holder

With a party hat for a base, this happy witch is the topper for a round goody box.

supplies
Small party hat
Staple remover
Craft foam in lime green, light pink, dark pink, white, black, purple, orange, and yellow

Pencil; scissors; stapler
Tracing paper
Pinking shears
Glue for foam and plastic
Paper punch
6 black pipe cleaners

Marking pen
Awl
Star paper punch
12-inch-long piece of
1½-inch-wide purple
grosgrain ribbon
Round papier-mâché
box

what to do

1 Remove staples from party hat. Lay hat flat on lime green foam. Trace the shape. Using the hat again as a pattern, trace around the top 2 inches of the hat point on black foam. Connect the sides with a U-shape scallop. Cut out the green and black pieces. Align the black foam over the tip of the green hat shape and staple where ends join. Staple the party hat back together. Place the green foam over the hat shape and staple at the seam to secure.

2 Enlarge and/or trace the patterns, *above right.* Cut out the shapes. Trace around the pattern pieces on the appropriate colors of craft foam. Cut out the shapes using scissors or pinking shears.

3 Glue the face pieces in place. Punch a hole from foam for the wart

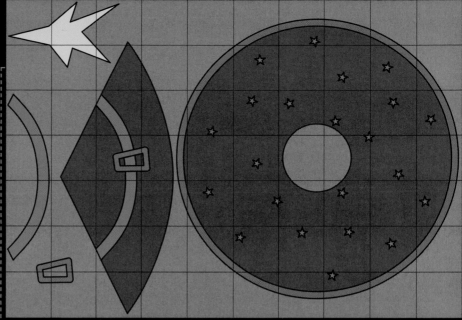

WITCH HAT PATTERNS 1 SQUARE = 1 INCH

**WITCH FACE
FULL-SIZE
PATTERNS**

on the nose. Glue in place. Let the glue dry.

4 Cut the pipe cleaners in half. Wrap around a medium-size marking pen and remove. Use an awl to poke holes in the top of the green cone, three on each side. Glue one end of each pipe cleaner inside a hole. Let dry.

5 Pull the foam brim over the hat point. Glue on the hatband, buckle, and star. Punch 30 stars from yellow foam. Glue on hat brim and in hair. Let dry.

6 Glue ribbon around papier-mâché box. Let dry.

terrifying trio

Papier-mâché boxes are just the right size to hold a handful of treats. This trio of characters uses bell, oval, and tree shapes.

supplies

Purchased papier-mâché boxes in bell, oval, and tree shapes
Acrylic paints in black, white, dark lime green, purple, and orange
Paintbrush; fan paintbrush
Crackle medium
Tracing paper
Pencil
Transfer paper
Pencil with round eraser
Round toothpick

what to do

1 For the skeleton, base-coat the bottom of the box white and the lid black as in Photo 1, right. Let dry. Apply a second coat and let dry.

2 Brush a thick coat of crackle medium over the painted areas. Let dry. To achieve the crackled look, paint black over the white without overlapping strokes. Paint the black lid white as shown in Photo 2. Let dry.

3 For all boxes, trace a pattern from *page 212*. Place transfer paper between pattern and box lid and retrace the pattern lines to transfer the design. Remove pattern and transfer paper.

4 Paint in the background areas, using the patterns as guides. Let the paint dry. Paint in the details. For large dots, such as the witch's eyes, dip the eraser of a pencil into paint and dot onto the surface. For small dots, dip a toothpick into paint and dot onto surface. To layer dots or other motifs, let paint dry between coats.

5 For the edge of the skeleton and the hair on the witch and dracula, use a fan brush. Using very little paint, make short strokes from the outer edge inward as shown in Photo 3 to achieve the desired effect. Let dry.

continued on page 212

1

2

3

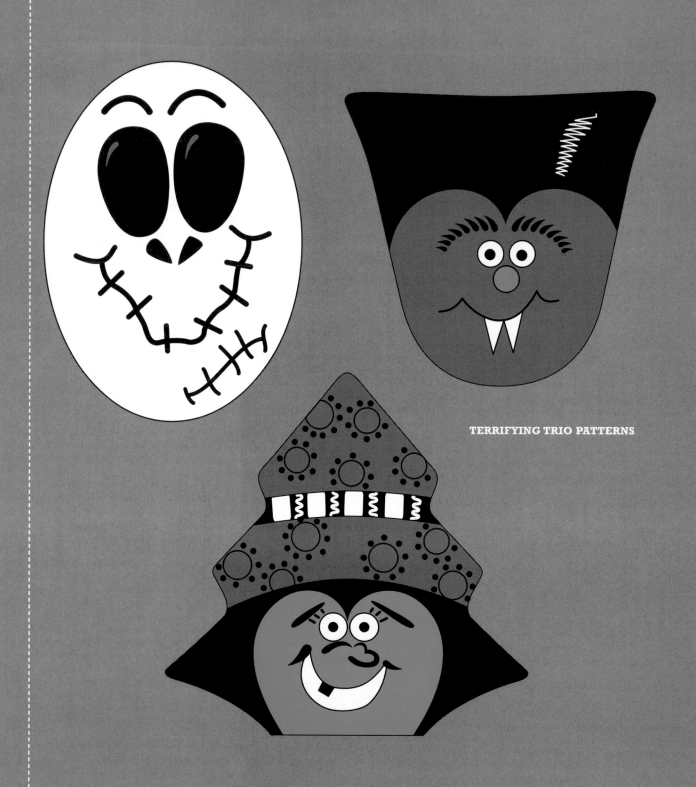

TERRIFYING TRIO PATTERNS

floral cone

Sequin hearts are arranged as dainty flowers on this pretty see-through treat cone.

supplies

Heart-shape sequins in orange and purple
Thick white crafts glue
Purchased acrylic cone (available at crafts stores)
Metallic gold beads
Paper punch
1 pink and 1 yellow pipe cleaner

what to do

1 Arrange five of the same color of sequins in a circle to form a flower shape. Glue in place. Glue orange and purple heart flowers randomly on the cone. Let dry.

2 Glue a gold bead in the center of each flower. Let the glue dry.

3 Punch a hole ½ inch from top of cone. Punch a second hole opposite the first. Twist two pipe cleaners together. Thread the pipe cleaners through the holes, securing to the cone by twisting the pipe cleaner ends upward. Shape the pipe cleaners into a handle.

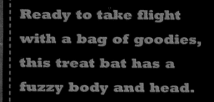

supplies

Tracing paper; pencil
Scissors; black paper
Fall-color papers
Black craft foam
Black marking pen
Thick white crafts glue
Green paper treat bag
Purple pom-poms
Plastic wiggly eyes
2 black pipe cleaners

*Ready to take flight
with a bag of goodies,
this treat bat has a
fuzzy body and head.*

what to do

1 Enlarge and trace patterns, *left,* onto tracing paper. Cut out and trace onto black and colored papers. Cut out leaves and bat wings. Cut ears from craft foam or paper.

2 Outline leaves and leaf veins with black marking pen. Glue leaves randomly on the bag.

3 Pleat bat wings as shown in the photo, *above left.* Glue purple pom-poms onto center of wings. Glue on eyes and ears. Poke holes in wings and insert black pipe cleaners to form legs.

LEAF PATTERNS   1 SQUARE = 1 INCH

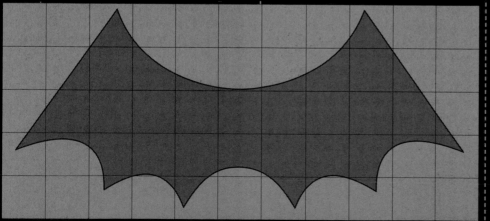

BAT WING PATTERN   1 SQUARE = 1 INCH

Treat guests right with one of these sticker-motif pails overflowing with candy.

painted pails

supplies
Newspapers
Metal pail
Matte black spray paint
Halloween stickers
Paintable glitter
Paintbrush
Shredded paper or
  polyester film
Halloween candy
Curling ribbon
Scissors

what to do

1 In a well-ventilated work area, cover work surface with newspapers. Place pail on newspapers. Lift the handle up. Spray-paint the interior of the pail. Paint the pail sides and handle. Let the paint dry. Apply a second coat of paint. Let dry.

2 Apply a Halloween sticker to one side of the pail. Smooth onto surface by gently rubbing with your finger.

3 Brush glitter over the handle and over the sticker, extending the glitter around the sticker in an irregular shape. Let the glitter dry.

4 Fill the pail with shred and candy.

5 Tie curling ribbon around the handle. Curl by pulling the ribbon tightly against scissors blade. Trim the ribbon ends if desired.

215

Start collecting glass jars to make these strikingly sturdy containers for Halloween sweets and snacks.

supplies
Glass jar
Etching cream
Paintbrush
Rubber gloves
Dish soap
Computer and printer
Colored papers in
   orange, purple, lime
   green, white, or yellow
Ruler; scissors; tape
Pipe cleaners in white,
   black, orange, yellow,
   purple, lime green,
   metallic gold, or
   metallic silver

what to do

1 Brush the exterior of the jar with etching cream as shown in Photo 1, *right.* Apply a thick, even coat, etching the jar according to the manufacturer's directions.

2 Put on rubber gloves. Thoroughly rinse off etching cream in a sink, as in Photo 2. Rinse sink well. Wash jar with dish soap. Let dry.

3 Using a computer, type MONSTER MIX, BOO, TRICK-OR-TREAT, or other Halloween words or phrases. Enlarge the type to fill the desired space, vertically or horizontally, on the jar. Print the word(s) on colored paper.

4 Measure the height of the jar and trim the paper to that size. Roll the paper strip and insert into the jar. If needed, trim the paper ends so they do not overlap the lettering. From the inside of the jar,

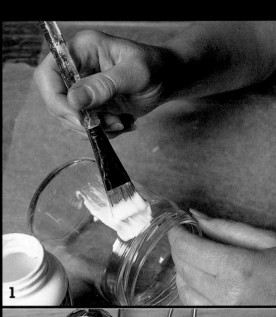

1

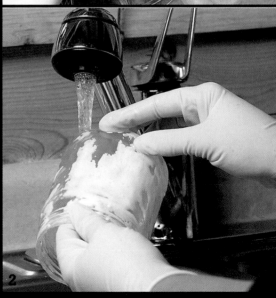

2

cookie treats

Hats off to these chocolate temptations made from ice cream cones and purchased cookies. For a sweet surprise, each cone is filled with candy treats before it is attached to the base. The instructions follow on page 220. For more cookie treat ideas, turn the page.

candy-filled witches' hats

supplies

Resealable plastic bag
16-ounce can of chocolate frosting
Scissors
20 chocolate ice cream cones
Candy corn or assorted small candies
20 2- to 3-inch chocolate cookies
Waxed paper
Large green and yellow gumdrops

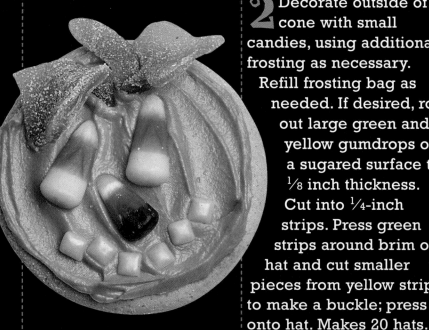

what to do

1 Fill a resealable plastic bag with some chocolate frosting. Seal bag, cut a very small end off one corner of the bag, and set aside. Invert cone and fill with about 2 tablespoons candy corn or small candies. Pipe some frosting from bag along bottom edge of cone. Press a cookie against frosting. Carefully place witch hat onto a baking sheet lined with waxed paper.

2 Decorate outside of cone with small candies, using additional frosting as necessary. Refill frosting bag as needed. If desired, roll out large green and yellow gumdrops on a sugared surface to $\frac{1}{8}$ inch thickness. Cut into $\frac{1}{4}$-inch strips. Press green strips around brim of hat and cut smaller pieces from yellow strips to make a buckle; press onto hat. Makes 20 hats.

sugar cookie fix-ups

supplies

Orange, yellow, and green paste food coloring
1 16-ounce can vanilla frosting
Purchased plain sugar cookies
Red, green, and yellow tubes of colored decorating frosting
Small candies

what to do

1 Add food coloring to purchased vanilla frosting to make orange, yellow, and green frosting. Spread frosting on sugar cookies and decorate with decorating frosting and small candies to make jack-o'-lanterns, ghosts, and monsters. See photos, *left* and *opposite,* for ideas.

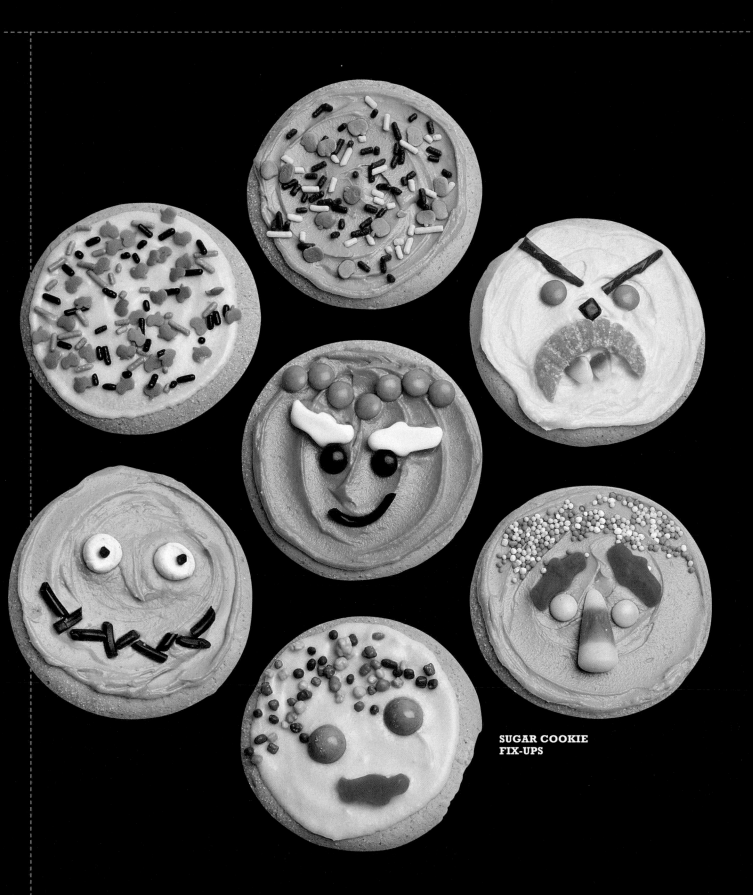

**SUGAR COOKIE
FIX-UPS**

jack -o'- lantern treat totes

Crepe paper is for more than just decorating ceilings! Cut small squares from the roll and decoupage the pieces over a balloon to create a pumpkin shell that's all ready to carve. Fill with shredded paper and wrapped goodies for little ones to enjoy. The instructions are on page 225.

supplies

Newspapers
Small balloons
Disposable foam plate
Crafts knife
Scissors
Orange crepe paper
Decoupage medium
Paintbrush
Small foam ball, such as
  Styrofoam
Colored papers in
  yellow, black, and
  purple
Thick white crafts glue
Small paper punch
Eyelets and eyelet tool
Plastic-coated wires in
  purple, black, white,
  orange, yellow,
  and green
Ice pick or skewer

what to do

1 Cover your work surface with newspapers. Blow up a balloon to about the size of a baseball. Secure the end.

2 Cut a small X in the center of the foam plate using a crafts knife. From the top of the plate, pull the knot of the balloon to the back of the plate. This will help hold the balloon while you work.

3 Use scissors to cut several squares from the crepe paper roll. Cover the bottom two-thirds of the balloon with a coat of decoupage medium. Place crepe paper squares over this area, using decoupage medium to stick the pieces to the balloon, as shown in Photo 1, *opposite.* Continue adding crepe paper squares until at least two layers cover the bottom two-thirds of the balloon. Brush a coat of decoupage medium over the crepe paper. Let it dry.

4 Pop the balloon and remove it. Place a foam ball inside the crepe paper cup. Use a crafts knife to cut a face in one side as shown in Photo 2.

5 Cut a circle or oval from colored paper to fit inside the crepe paper cup behind the cut features, as shown in Photo 3. Glue the paper in place and let the glue dry.

6 Punch a hole on each side of the face, approximately 1 inch from the top. Insert an eyelet in each hole and secure it using the eyelet tool as shown in Photo 4.

7 Braid or twist wires together to make a handle. Insert the wire ends through the eyelet holes. To coil the wire ends, wrap them around an ice pick or skewer.

halloween brews

Whether you're chilled to the bone or in need of a cool potion, try one of these delicious concoctions. The Hot Golden Cider, top left, has a caramel-flavored candy stirring stick. The other warmer-upper, Haunting Hot Chocolate, has a marshmallow ghost garnish. Or cool off with a cup of red Transylvania Punch that tastes of cherry and lemon-lime. The last of the cold brews, Orange Cream Punch, includes sherbet to make it a frosty delight. The recipes are on pages 228–229.

hot golden cider

supplies

6 cups apple cider
2 12½-ounce cans apricot nectar
2 tablespoons packed brown sugar
100-percent-cotton cheesecloth
Scissors
6-inch-long cinnamon sticks
½ teaspoon whole cloves
Cotton string
Caramel-flavored candy stick, optional

what to do

1 In a large saucepan combine apple cider, apricot nectar, and brown sugar. Cut a double thickness of 100-percent-cotton cheesecloth into an 8-inch square. Combine cinnamon sticks and cloves in cheesecloth. Bring up corners of cheesecloth and tie with cotton string. Place in saucepan. Bring mixture to boiling; reduce heat. Simmer, covered, for 10 minutes.

2 Remove and discard spices. Serve warm. Garnish with caramel-flavored candy stick, if desired. Makes twelve 6-ounce servings.

orange cream punch

supplies

1 14-ounce can sweetened condensed milk
1 12-ounce can frozen orange juice concentrate, thawed
Orange food coloring
2 1-liter bottles club soda or ginger ale, chilled
Orange sherbet

what to do

1 In a punch bowl combine sweetened condensed milk and orange juice concentrate. Tint with orange food coloring, if desired. Add club soda or ginger ale.

2 Top with scoops of orange sherbet. Serve immediately. Makes thirty-two 6-ounce servings.

ORANGE CREAM PUNCH

haunting hot chocolate

supplies

1 medium orange
3 cups whole milk
⅔ cup vanilla-flavored baking pieces or candy coating
⅛ teaspoon ground nutmeg
1 teaspoon vanilla
Purchased marshmallow ghosts
Whipped cream, optional
Ground nutmeg, optional

what to do

1 Remove peel of orange with vegetable peeler; set orange aside.

2 In a medium saucepan combine orange peel, $\frac{1}{4}$ cup of the milk, vanilla-flavored baking pieces, and nutmeg; whisk over low heat until baking pieces are melted.

Remove orange peel. Whisk in remaining milk and heat through. Remove from heat. Stir in vanilla.

3 Serve warm in mugs. Top with a marshmallow ghost, dollop with whipped cream, and sprinkle with nutmeg, if desired. Makes five 6-ounce servings.

HAUNTING HOT CHOCOLATE

transylvania punch

supplies

2 cups water

1 3-ounce package cherryflavored gelatin

4 12-ounce cans lemon-lime or ginger ale carbonated beverage, chilled

what to do

1 In a medium saucepan bring 2 cups water to boiling. Transfer to a bowl. Add gelatin and stir until gelatin is dissolved. Cover and chill 4 hours or overnight.

2 To serve, pour about $\frac{1}{2}$ cup of carbonated beverage into a glass. Spoon in an equal amount of the chilled gelatin. Gelatin should float on carbonated beverage. If desired, stir together just before drinking. Makes six 6-ounce servings.

puzzle cookies

Purchased cookie dough is the key to creating these puzzling Halloween sweets.

supplies

¼ **cup all-purpose flour**
1 **18-ounce roll refrigerated sugar cookie dough**
3- **to 4-inch Halloween cookie cutter**
1 **recipe Egg Yolk Paint**

what to do

1 In a medium bowl knead flour into sugar cookie dough. Divide dough into 6 portions. On an ungreased cookie sheet pat each portion into a 5-inch square. Press a well-floured 3- to 4-inch Halloween cookie cutter into the center of the square (use smaller cutters if desired). Carefully remove cookie cutter without removing dough. Using a table knife, cut outside portion of square into large puzzle pieces.

2 Brush dough puzzle pieces with different colors of Egg Yolk Paint.

3 Bake in a 350° oven for 7 to 8 minutes or until bottoms of cookies just start to brown and centers are set. While still warm, carefully recut pieces with the cookie cutter and knife. Trim edges as needed. Transfer cookies to a wire rack; cool completely. Makes 6 puzzle cookies.

Egg Yolk Paint: In a small mixing bowl beat 2 egg yolks and 2 teaspoons water. Divide mixture among 3 to 4 small bowls. In each bowl, add 2 to 3 drops of liquid food coloring or desired amount of paste food coloring; mix well. Apply with small, clean paintbrush. If mixture thickens while standing, stir in water, one drop at a time.

An all-time kids' favorite, these adorable chain rattlers have a cereal and marshmallow base and are coated with vanilla-flavored candy. Have fun making different shapes of ghosts and experimenting with candy bits to create a variety of ghastly, ghostly expressions.

eat-'em-up ghosts

supplies
- 1 10-ounce bag of marshmallows
- ¼ cup margarine or butter
- 6 cups crisp rice cereal
- 12 ounces vanilla-flavored candy coating, melted
- Black licorice candies
- Chocolate sprinkles
- Miniature semisweet chocolate pieces

what to do

1 In a large pot combine marshmallows and margarine. Cook and stir over medium-low heat until mixture is melted. Gradually stir in cereal until well combined.

2 Use ½ to 1 cup of the cereal mixture per ghost to form into ghost shapes. Set aside to cool completely.

3 Dip each ghost shape into melted candy coating. Use pieces of licorice, chocolate sprinkles, and/or chocolate pieces for the eyes, nose, eyebrows, and mouth. Makes 9 to 12 ghosts.

Even though it looks spooky, this imaginative forest is completely edible.

haunted forest platter

supplies

3 stalks of broccoli
3 medium beets
Wood toothpicks
3 hard-boiled eggs
Ripe olives, pimiento-
stuffed olives, and/or
tiny sweet pickles
Assorted vegetables,
such as cherry
tomatoes, pea pods,
kohlrabies, radishes,
red sweet peppers, and
yellow sweet peppers,
Shredded carrot
Liquid green food
coloring
1 ounce spaghetti,
cooked and drained

what to do

1 To make a haunted forest, first create trees. Cut bottoms from stalks of broccoli to make 6-inch broccoli trees. Slice beets about $\frac{1}{2}$ to $\frac{3}{4}$ inch thick to make a base for broccoli trees. Break wood toothpicks in half. Insert three to four toothpick pieces into bottom of each broccoli stalk and then insert into a beet slice. Stand broccoli upright. Cover to keep moist.

2 To make egg ghosts, use a small knife or $\frac{1}{2}$-inch aspic cutters to hollow out eyes and mouths to form a face. Cut small pieces of ripe olive to press into hollowed-out areas for eyes or mouth, if desired. Cover to keep moist.

3 Using your imagination, create creepy creatures with assorted vegetables, olives, and/or pickles.

4 Place broccoli trees on serving platter. Cover surface of platter with shredded carrot. Hide egg ghosts in forest along with creepy creatures. Scatter piles of assorted vegetables. Add strips of red sweet pepper to the broccoli branches.

5 To make moss, add a few drops of green food coloring to a small amount of water in a medium bowl. Add cooked spaghetti and let stand about 5 minutes. Drain and place over broccoli trees. Keep platter covered until serving time. If necessary, spritz platter with water to keep it moist.

what to do

1 Place 2 packages of cream cheese, taco-flavored cheese, and margarine in a mixing bowl. Let stand at room temperature for 30 minutes. Add milk to the cheese mixture. Beat with an electric mixer on medium speed until combined, stopping the mixer occasionally to scrape the bowl with a rubber spatula. Cover bowl and chill 4 to 24 hours.

2 Form into a head shape and place on a serving plate. In a bowl stir together the 2 packages of softened cream cheese until smooth. Spread head with softened cream cheese. Press in tortilla chips for ears. Using toothpicks, attach a pickled pepper for nose, pimiento-stuffed olives for eyes, and pepper-stuffed olives for toes. Cut zigzag peppers for eyebrows. Use shredded beets for hair and press in carrot sticks for teeth. Serve with assorted crackers. Makes 20 servings.

This little goblin won't bite you even if you nibble on him! The yummy cheese spreads easily on crackers for a quick snack.

supplies

2 8-ounce packages cream cheese
1 8-ounce package shredded taco-flavored cheese
¼ cup margarine or butter
2 tablespoons milk
2 8-ounce packages cream cheese, softened
Tortilla chips
Toothpicks
Pickled pepper
Pimiento-stuffed olives
Red pepper-stuffed olives
Green sweet pepper
Shredded beets
Carrot sticks
Assorted crackers

Topped with Halloween sprinkles, this mouthwatering cheesecake is edged in orange-colored candy coating.

spooky cheesecake

supplies
3 ounces
  vanilla-flavored
  candy coating
Orange paste food
  coloring
1 8-ounce container
  frozen whipped dessert
  topping, thawed
1 purchased frozen
  cheesecake, thawed
  (1 pound, 14 ounces)
Small multicolored
  decorative Halloween
  candies

what to do
1 In a small saucepan melt candy coating. Add orange food coloring to desired shade. Transfer to a baking sheet lined with waxed paper. Spread to an 11×8-inch rectangle. Chill in refrigerator until firm (about 30 minutes). Break into small shards. Set aside.

2 Reserve ½ cup of dessert topping; set aside. Pipe or spread remaining topping over surface of cheesecake.

Sprinkle with Halloween candies. Attach shards of candy coating to the edge of cheesecake with reserved dessert topping. Makes 12 servings.

gumdrop pumpkins

Cut, press, cut, press, and have these darling little pumpkins to help you celebrate at trick-or-treat time. Use them as party favors by placing several gumdrop goodies in a small crate, papier-mâché box, or basket lined with crimped, shredded paper. Tuck in a plastic spider ring as the frightful finishing element.

supplies
Orange slice-shape jelly candies
Small green gumdrops

what to do
1 To make pumpkins, trim the edges of two jelly candies to create straight sides. Push the two sticky sides together, forming a pumpkin shape.

2 Cut a small piece from the bottom of a small green gumdrop. Press into the top of candy pumpkin.

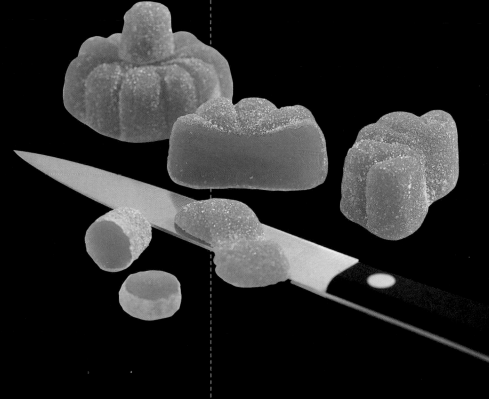

beetle juice slush

supplies

1 46-ounce can apricot nectar
1 12-ounce can orange juice concentrate, thawed
2 16-ounce packages unsweetened sliced peaches, thawed
7 12-ounce cans lemon-lime carbonated beverage, chilled

This tasty concoction is fit for ghouls and boys of all ages.

what to do

1 In a food processor bowl or blender container, add one-third each of the apricot nectar, orange juice concentrate, and sliced peaches. Cover and process or blend until smooth. Pour into a freezer container. Repeat with the remaining nectar, orange juice, and peaches. Cover and seal mixture. Freeze until firm.

2 Scrape about ½ cup of the mixture into each 10-ounce glass. Add an equal amount of carbonated beverage. Stir to combine. Makes 20 servings.

Note: *Wash one-piece plastic toys before adding to slush; remove before drinking.*

This salad may look slimy but it's really delicious!

buggy pasta

supplies

- 4 ounces fusilli (twisted spaghetti)
- 4 ounces spaghetti
- 1 medium yellow squash and/or zucchini, halved lengthwise and sliced
- 1 cup small cherry tomatoes
- 1 cup fresh pea pods, tips and strings removed
- 1 cup pitted ripe olives
- 1 cup pimiento-stuffed olives
- 1 cup cubed smoked cheddar cheese or cheddar cheese (4 ounces)
- 1 cup unblanched whole almonds, toasted
- ½ cup thinly sliced green onions (4)
- 1 cup regular or nonfat Italian salad dressing (8 ounces)

what to do

1 Cook fusilli and spaghetti according to the package directions. Drain, rinse with cold water, and drain again.

2 In a large bowl combine fusilli and spaghetti and remaining ingredients except dressing. Add dressing to the fusilli mixture; toss gently to coat. Cover and chill 2 to 24 hours. Makes 12 side dish servings.

3 To serve the pasta Halloween-style, place it in a clean plastic cauldron embellished with well-secured plastic spiders.

finger foods

These quick-fix finger sandwiches will have everyone biting their nails. Pair them with miniature gravestones for a wonderfully edible duo.

tombstone sandwiches

supplies
Hot dog bun
Ham salad
Squeeze bottle mustard
  and catsup

what to do
1 Cut a hot dog bun in half crosswise. Fill the inside of bun with your favorite ham salad. Using squeeze bottle mustard and catsup, mark front of buns with crosses and R.I.P. letters to make tombstones. Stand upright on a serving platter. Makes 2 sandwiches.

edible fingers

supplies
Thinly sliced
  firm-textured bread
Chicken salad
Sliced almonds
Cream cheese, softened

what to do
1 Remove crust from two slices of bread. Spread some of your favorite chicken salad onto one of the slices. Top with the other slice of bread. Cut lengthwise into ¾-inch-wide strips. With a small knife, taper one end of each strip to form a point. Attach a sliced almond to this end with some softened cream cheese to make fingernails.

Imaginations will soar when partygoers hear the name of this sizzling pizza.

body parts pizza

supplies

- 8 ounces skinless, boneless chicken breasts
- 1 tablespoon cooking oil
- 1 medium red onion, sliced
- 1 16-ounce Italian bread shell, such as focaccia
- 1 cup purchased Alfredo sauce
- 1 small green sweet pepper, cut into strips
- 1 tomato, cut into wedges
- 1 5.3-ounce package cocktail wieners
- 1 6-ounce jar marinated artichoke hearts, drained
- 2 tablespoons shredded Parmesan cheese

what to do

1 Cut chicken breasts into strips. In a medium skillet heat cooking oil over medium heat. Add chicken and cook, turning occasionally, about 5 minutes or until chicken strips are golden brown and no longer pink on the inside. Remove from skillet and set aside. Add onion to skillet, using additional oil if necessary. Cook over medium heat about 8 minutes or until onion is tender.

2 Place bread shell on a pizza pan or baking sheet. Spread Alfredo sauce over shell. Top with chicken strips, onion, pepper strips, tomato wedges, cocktail wieners, and artichoke hearts. Sprinkle with Parmesan cheese. Bake in a 425° oven for 10 to 15 minutes. Makes 12 to 16 servings.

spooks on a stick

Cookies—especially ones decorated for the bewitching season are so much more fun to eat when presented on a stick!

supplies

Chopped vanilla- and chocolate-flavored candy coating
Orange, green, violet, or yellow paste food coloring
Wood skewers
Crème sandwich cookies
Assorted small candies and nuts

what to do

1 Melt small amounts of chopped vanilla- and chocolate-flavored candy coating in separate containers. If desired, add orange, green, violet, or yellow paste food coloring to the vanilla candy coating. Insert a wood skewer into one end of each crème sandwich cookie. If cookie begins to open too much, add some melted candy coating to the inside of cookie sandwich, press together around skewer, and chill in refrigerator until firm.

2 Working with one cookie at a time, dip cookie into melted coating, covering completely. Transfer to a cookie sheet lined with waxed paper. While coating is still soft, decorate with small candies and nuts, making ghosts, skeletons, witches, pumpkins, monsters, mummies, and owls.

sticks mix

Sticks and stones may break your bones but this snack will never hurt you. Use the ingredients listed here or try mixing your own special combination.

supplies
Pretzel sticks
Sweetened, fruit-flavored round toasted cereal
Chocolate-flavored puffed corn cereal
Cheese-flavored snacks
Orange and brown candy-coated milk chocolate pieces

what to do
1 Add all ingredients together. Stir gently to mix.
2 Place individual servings in cereal bowls or place mix in one large serving bowl. To serve Halloween-style, place mix in a clean trick-or-treat pail.

Whether you start with a purchased cake or bake your own, these little creatures devour each morsel.

the rat cake

supplies

1 2-layer white cake mix
Violet, orange, green, and yellow paste food coloring
3 ounces vanilla-flavored candy coating, chopped
Small heavy plastic resealable bags
2 16-ounce cans vanilla frosting
Nontoxic rubber or plastic mice, rats, snakes, bats, and spiders

what to do

1 Prepare cake mix according to package directions. If desired, add orange or green food coloring to batter. Cool.

2 Divide candy coating into three custard cups. Microwave, one at a time, on high for 1 minute or until softened. Stir until melted. Stir a small amount of violet, orange, or green food coloring into each. Cool slightly. Place each in a resealable bag. Seal and cut the tip from one corner. Line a cookie sheet with waxed paper. Make spirals and squiggles on the paper. Chill in refrigerator until set. Keep refrigerated.

3 Tint frosting with yellow and green food coloring for lime green.

4 Wash and dry all animals. Assemble and frost cake. Decorate as desired. Makes 1 cake (12 servings).

witch hat cake

Five layers of round cakes support a pointed ice cream cone to make this towering witch hat.

supplies

1 2-layer white cake mix
Green or orange food coloring, optional
1 rolled sugar ice cream cone
2 16-ounce cans chocolate fudge frosting
8-inch wood skewer
Halloween candies and/or large yellow and white gumdrops

what to do

1 Grease and flour one 9×1½-inch round baking pan and one 9×9×2-inch square baking pan. Prepare cake mix according to package directions, adding green or orange food coloring to batter, if desired.

Remove from pans and cool on wire racks. Trim tops of cakes to make even thickness.

2 Cut a 5-, 3½-, 2½-, and 2-inch circle from the square cake layer. Fill the ice cream cone with cake scraps.

3 Place a small amount of frosting in the middle of a cake plate. Place the 9-inch round cake layer on frosting and press gently to secure.

4 Place about ⅓ cup of the frosting in the center of cake layer and spread to a 5-inch circle. Place the 5-inch cake circle on top. Spread about ¼ cup frosting in the center of this cake layer and top with the 3½-inch cake circle. Spread more frosting and add the 2½- and 2-inch cake layers. Insert an 8-inch wood skewer down through the cake layers for added support. Attach the ice cream cone on top with additional frosting.

5 Frost cake and ice cream cone with remaining frosting (see tip, *right*). Decorate as desired with candies and/or gumdrops. Makes 1 cake (12 servings).

Gumdrop Moons and Stars: Use a rolling pin to roll out gumdrops on sugar-coated waxed paper. Cut out moon and star shapes with hors d'oeuvre cutters. Dip cutters in sugar to prevent sticking.

To spread frosting more easily onto sides of cake: Fill a small resealable plastic bag with about 1 cup frosting. Snip off one corner and pipe frosting onto cake sides. Spread evenly.

snake bites

Complete with olive eyes, this slithering fellow is so realistic that you expect him to hiss.

supplies
3   16-ounce loaves frozen white bread dough, thawed
6   tablespoons brown mustard
16 ounces thinly sliced ham
12 ounces thinly sliced salami
6   ounces provolone cheese, shredded
6   ounces mozzarella cheese, shredded
3   egg yolks
3   teaspoons water
Green, red, and yellow liquid food coloring
3   tablespoons grated Parmesan cheese, optional
2   whole cloves
2   small pimiento-stuffed olives
Toothpicks
Bottled roasted red sweet pepper strip (6×1 inch)
Bamboo leaves, optional

what to do

1 Line three cookie sheets with foil, grease the foil, and set aside. Roll one of the loaves of dough on a lightly floured surface to a 26×6-inch rectangle. Allow dough to rest a few minutes while rolling. Lightly brush 2 tablespoons mustard to within 1 inch of the sides of dough. Layer one-third of the ham and salami over mustard. Mix together provolone and mozzarella cheeses. Sprinkle one-third of the cheese mixture over ham and salami. Brush edges of dough with water. Roll up into a spiral, starting with one of the long sides. Pinch all edges to seal. Shape dough on prepared cookie sheet in an S shape.

2 Combine one of the egg yolks, 1 teaspoon water, and several drops of one food coloring. Repeat to make green, red, and yellow egg wash. Paint stripes crosswise over loaf, allowing the wash to drizzle down sides.

3 Let loaf rise in a warm place for about 20 minutes. Sprinkle top of loaf with 1 tablespoon of the Parmesan cheese, if desired.

4 While one section of the snake rises, repeat with remaining bread dough and ingredients. Taper one end of two loaves to a rounded point to make a head and tail. Insert 2 whole cloves at head end, making nostrils. Place on prepared cookie sheets. Paint and let rise as above.

5 Bake snake sections in a 375° oven for 25 to 30 minutes or until bottoms of loaves are golden. Insert olives with toothpicks above the cloves to form eyes. Use pepper strip to make forked tongue. Assemble snake sections on bamboo leaves, if desired. Slice and serve warm. Makes 24 slices.

Satisfy a snack attack with Spinal Cord Spirals, Fried Gremlin Ears, Oozing Eyeballs, and Gooey Green Pods— if you dare!

spinal cord spirals

supplies

1   8-ounce package cream cheese, softened
4   8-inch flour tortillas
2   cups spinach leaves or 4 leaf lettuce leaves
2   tomatoes, thinly sliced
6   ounces thinly sliced pepperoni or salami
1   8-ounce package shredded mozzarella cheese (2 cups)
Toothpicks

what to do

1 Spread 3 tablespoons of the cream cheese to within 1 inch of the edge of a tortilla. Layer with some of the spinach leaves, tomato slices, pepperoni, and ½ cup of mozzarella cheese. Tightly roll up into a spiral. Repeat with remaining ingredients.

2 To serve, transfer to a cutting board. Slice off and discard ends. Cut rolls into 1-inch slices. Secure with toothpicks. Stack three or four spirals, slightly off center, to look like a spinal column. Makes 24.

fried gremlin ears

supplies

1   9-ounce package fresh or frozen cheese-filled tortellini
Green food coloring, optional
1   egg, beaten
¼   cup milk
½   cup Italian-seasoned fine dry bread crumbs
2   tablespoons grated Parmesan cheese
Cooking oil
Spaghetti sauce, optional

what to do

1 Cook tortellini according to package directions. Drain in a colander, rinse, drain again, and cool. If

desired, fill a large bowl with cold water and add several drops of green food coloring. Add cooked pasta; let stand 15 to 20 minutes. Drain well. Combine egg and milk in a large bowl. Add tortellini and toss gently to coat. Combine bread crumbs and Parmesan cheese in a plastic bag. Lift tortellini with a slotted spoon and add about one-fourth at a time to bread crumb mixture. Toss to coat with crumbs. Remove.

2 Add about 12 tortellini to deep, hot oil (365°). Fry for 1 minute or until golden brown. Remove with a slotted spoon and drain on paper towels. Transfer to a cookie sheet and keep warm in a 300° oven while frying remaining tortellini. Serve warm with spaghetti sauce if desired. Makes 78 ears.

oozing eyeballs

supplies

1 1½-pound spaghetti squash
3 tablespoons bottled ranch salad dressing

24 large cherry tomatoes
24 pimiento-stuffed olives

what to do

1 Cut squash in half lengthwise; remove seeds. Place squash halves cut side down in a baking dish. Bake in a 350° oven for 30 to 40 minutes or until tender. Or place halves cut side down in a microwave-safe baking dish with ¼ cup water. Microwave, covered, on high 17 minutes or until tender, turning once.

2 Using a fork, scrape squash to make long shreds. You should have about 2 cups cooked squash. Place squash in a bowl; stir in salad dressing. Cut off tops of cherry tomatoes. Use a small spoon to hollow out tomatoes. Fill centers with cooked squash. Place a pimiento-stuffed olive in the center of the cooked squash in each tomato. Cover and chill up to 4 hours before serving. Makes 24 servings.

gooey green pods

supplies

24 pea pods
1 8-ounce tub cream cheese with garlic and herbs
2 tablespoons finely chopped carrot
2 tablespoons finely chopped red sweet pepper
2 tablespoons finely chopped green sweet pepper

what to do

1 Remove tips and strings from pea pods. Cut open one long side of each pea pod. Set aside. In a small bowl stir together remaining ingredients. Place cream cheese mixture in a small resealable plastic bag. Close bag. Cut off one corner from bag and squeeze mixture into open pods. Makes 24.

bat wings

Tell the kids they're eating bat wings and they will request them even when it's not Halloween!

supplies

20 **chicken wings (3½ pounds)**
½   **cup soy sauce**
2   **teaspoons grated fresh ginger or**
    ½ teaspoon ground ginger
¼   **teaspoon crushed red pepper**
1   **teaspoon five-spice powder**
2   **cloves garlic, minced**
1   **recipe Swamp Dip**

what to do

1 Place wings in a plastic bag set in a shallow dish. In a small bowl stir together soy sauce, ginger, crushed red pepper, five-spice powder, and garlic to make marinade. Pour over wings. Close bag and toss to coat. Chill in refrigerator several hours or overnight, turning bag occasionally. Remove wings from bag, reserving the marinade.

2 Place wings on a 15×10×1-inch baking pan lined with foil. Bake, uncovered, in a 450° oven for 10 minutes. Brush with reserved marinade (discard remaining marinade). Bake 15 to 20 minutes longer or until chicken is tender and no longer pink. Serve with Swamp Dip. Makes 20 appetizers.

Swamp Dip: In a small bowl stir together an 8-ounce container of dairy sour cream and 3 tablespoons coarse ground mustard. Garnish with fresh whole chives.

supplies for the pumpkin

Pumpkin
Spoon
Bat cookie cutter
Sharp paring knife
Candle
Matches

what to do

1 Cut off the top of a pumpkin. Scoop out the insides.

2 Press a bat cookie cutter randomly into the pumpkin, making an impression through the pumpkin skin. Use a sharp paring knife to carve the bat shapes. Insert a candle, replace the lid, and light the candle through one of the openings. Never leave burning candles unattended.

ghosts and ghouls house

Constructing this haunted house provides an opportunity for the kids to join in. You supply all the ingredients and watch them search their imaginations to make the edible house even more scary.

supplies

1   16-ounce can
    chocolate frosting
Resealable plastic
    bags
16 honey graham
    cracker squares
1   clean 1-quart
    wax-coated paper
    milk carton
Serrated knife
4   chocolate graham
    cracker squares
7   black licorice twists
Small Halloween
    candy figures
Small candies
Orange and yellow
    decorating sugars
Green and yellow tube
    gel frosting

what to do

1 Spoon some chocolate frosting into a plastic bag. Snip off one small corner. Fill bag with more frosting as needed. Pipe frosting from bag onto one side of a honey graham cracker square and press against one side of milk carton, even with bottom. Repeat with two more squares to cover one side. Repeat on remaining three sides. Cut two honey graham cracker squares diagonally from both bottom corners to center of top to form two triangle pieces for top of house; trim to fit. Pipe frosting on one side of both pieces and press into place on carton. Pipe frosting on one side of two chocolate graham cracker squares and press onto top of milk carton for roof. Pipe frosting onto corners of house. Press licorice twists in place.

2 To form a door, halve a chocolate graham cracker square and use frosting to attach one rectangle to the front bottom of house. Cut two honey graham cracker squares into two rectangles each. Pipe frosting around door and attach three of the rectangles to form an entryway. Cut small pieces of chocolate crackers for shutters. Pipe frosting onto one side of shutters and Halloween candy figures. Press onto sides of house for windows.

3 Decorate with candies, sugars, and gel frosting, as desired.

witches' broomsticks

supplies

12 7-inch pretzel rods,
    ³/₈ inch thick
6   pieces fruit-flavored
    licorice twists
Cherry or apricot
    rolled fruit leather
Black or red licorice
    string

what to do

1 Cut pretzel rods to 6 inches with a serrated knife. Quarter licorice twists lengthwise and then cut into 2-inch pieces. Place about 10 pieces around the cut end of a pretzel rod. Using an 8×1-inch piece of fruit leather, tightly wrap around the end of pretzel, securing the fruit licorice to the pretzel, and press fruit leather in place. Tie with a small piece of licorice string. Snip ends of fruit licorice with scissors to form broom fringe. Makes 12.

terrorific parties

and games

fiendishly fun ideas to celebrate Halloween

scare-me-silly invites

Start the party right with handmade invitations.

supplies for the cat invite

Tracing paper
Pencil
Scissors
Craft papers in black, yellow, and white
Glue stick
4×5¼-inch brown kraft postcard
¾-inch round red sticker
Marking pens in silver and black

what to do for the cat invite

1 Trace head and face patterns, *page 262,* onto tracing paper and cut out. The silver and black lines will be drawn with marking pens. Trace around head and pupil patterns on black paper,

eyes on yellow, and teeth on white. Cut out.

2 Glue black head shape to center of postcard. Attach yellow eyes, black pupils, and white teeth. Apply a red sticker to make the nose.

3 Use a black marking pen to draw in teeth lines, stars, dots, and swirls as shown on

pattern. Use a silver pen to draw in whiskers and lines in eyes. Color in stars and one tooth. Make silver dots on top of black dots and in the center of swirls.

4 Write party information on back side of the postcard.

supplies for the skeleton invite

Tracing paper
Pencil; scissors
Glue stick
Marking pens in silver and black
Craft papers in black, white, orange, and yellow; ruler
Round reinforcement stickers in yellow, purple, and green
Small round green stickers

what to do for the skeleton invite

1 Trace the patterns, *page 262,* onto tracing paper and cut out. The silver and black lines will be drawn with marking pens. Fold a piece of black paper in half, bringing the short ends together. Trace around the pattern for card shape on the folded piece of black paper. Trace around the bow tie shape on orange paper and the skeleton head on white. Cut out shapes. Cut a $3\frac{3}{4}\times\frac{5}{8}$-inch strip from yellow paper.

2 Glue the head shape approximately $\frac{1}{4}$ inch from the top of the card. Use the silver pen to draw in the arms and ribs.

3 Apply reinforcements and green stickers to the bow tie as desired. Trim or fold under stickers that hang over the edge of the bow tie. Glue the bow tie to the bottom of the head. Glue the yellow paper strip to the bottom of the card.

4 Use black pen to draw in face details and lettering. On the inside write AND SOMEWHERE TO GO! with a silver pen. Draw the details to the eyes using the silver pen.

5 Write the invitation information on the inside of the card.

supplies for the "come if you dare" invite

$5\frac{1}{2}\times8\frac{1}{2}$-inch piece of purple paper
Glue stick
$3\frac{3}{4}\times5$-inch piece of black paper
Computer and computer paper or magazines to make lettering
Scissors
Black marking pen

what to do for the "come if you dare" invite

1 Fold the purple paper in half, bringing the short ends together. Using the photo, *opposite,* as a guide, glue the black piece of paper onto one side of the purple paper at an angle.

2 To make the words, use a computer to print each word in a different font. Make the word PLEASE approximately $\frac{1}{4}$ inch high. Make the remaining words and exclamation point between $\frac{1}{2}$ and $1\frac{1}{8}$ inches high. If a computer is not available, clip the letters or entire words from magazines. Glue the words in place.

3 Write the party information on the inside of the card.

continued on page 262

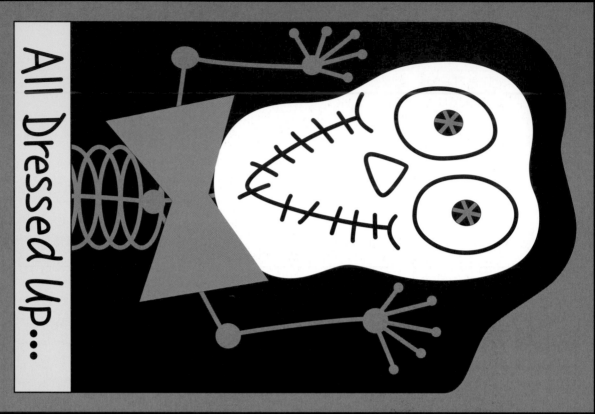

All Dressed Up...

SKELETON INVITE PATTERN

CAT INVITE PATTERN

spider salutations

These little fellows give recipients the creeps as they announce an upcoming monster bash.

supplies
Scissors; ruler
Card stock in orange or black
Crafts knife
Scrapbook papers in Halloween colors and designs; glue stick
$1/8$-inch round paper punch
28-gauge orange wire
Miniature black plastic spiders
Thick white crafts glue

what to do

1 Cut an $8^1/_2 \times 4^1/_4$-inch piece of card stock. Fold it in half to make a square card.

2 Using a crafts knife, cut a $2^1/_4 \times 2^1/_4$-inch window in the front of the card. Glue a $4^1/_4$-inch square of patterned scrapbook paper into the inside of the card with glue stick. Punch a hole through the center of card cover just above the window. Let the glue dry.

3 Cut a 2-inch length of wire. Hook one end of the wire through the hole. Bend the wire into the desired shape and then glue the spider to the other end of the wire. Or use crafts glue to attach the spider to the card cover just under the cut window. Let the glue dry.

rattling bones invite

Guests know they're in for the party of a lifetime when they receive this can of bones in the mail.

supplies

White air-dry clay, such as Crayola Model Magic; paper clip
Pencil; computer
Medium-weight paper in purple, orange, and lime green; scissors
Ruler; thick white crafts glue
New quart paint cans
Clear packing tape

what to do

1 To make each bone, roll a finger-size piece of clay, the center portion narrower than the ends. Pinch the ends slightly and make a notch in each end with a paper clip. Make six to eight bones for each invitation. Let the clay dry.

2 To make a skull, form a small pear shape from clay. With the larger end at the top, use a pencil point to make nasal cavities. Press your little finger into the clay above the nostrils to make eye sockets. To make the smile, draw a wide U with a pencil. Press the end of a paper clip along the U to complete. Let dry.

3 On a computer, type an invitation on lime green paper, leaving 1 inch at the top. Make the invitation small enough to fit inside the can. Glue the green paper onto orange paper. Trim ⅛ inch beyond the green edge. Glue the orange paper onto purple paper. Trim ¼ inch beyond the orange edge. Glue a bone to the top. Let dry. Using orange paper, write a mailing label. Wrap the label around the can and tape the ends together. Trace the lid on purple paper. Cut out ¼ inch within the line and glue to the lid. Let dry.

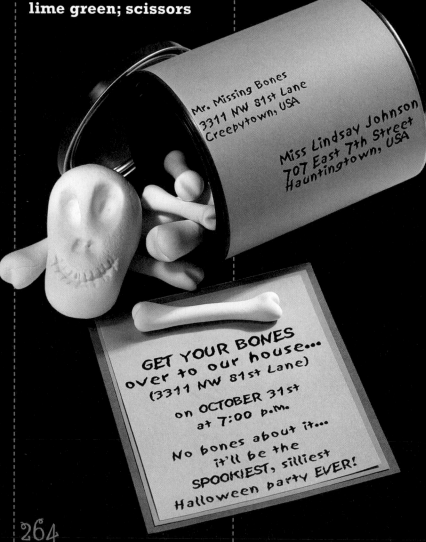

Mr. Missing Bones
3311 NW 81st Lane
Creepytown, USA

Miss Lindsay Johnson
707 East 7th Street
Hauntingtown, USA

GET YOUR BONES over to our house... (3311 NW 81st Lane)

on OCTOBER 31st at 7:00 p.m.

No bones about it... it'll be the SPOOKIEST, silliest Halloween party EVER!

confetti cards

supplies

**Medium-weight paper in
black, orange, white,
and purple**
Ruler
Pencil
Scissors
Glue stick
**Strong adhesive,
such as E6000**
Toothpick
**Plastic confetti in star,
bat, jack-o'-lantern,
witch, ghost, moon,
and circle shapes**
Silver marking pen

what to do

1 Cut the black or
orange background
paper to measure
5×10 inches. The fold for
these cards can be at the
top or the left as desired.

2 Cut the next square
layer from black or
orange to measure
4×4 inches. Use glue stick
to adhere the black
square atop the orange
card (window design) and
the orange square
atop the black card
(diamond design).

3 For the window
design, cut four
1½×1½-inch squares from
white and glue to card in
a window fashion as
shown, *above*. For the
diamond design, cut four

1½×1½-inch squares
from purple and glue to
card in a diamond pattern
as shown, *above*.

4 Use a toothpick to
apply a dot of strong
adhesive to the back of
each confetti piece before
placing on card. For stars,
cut some in half to align
with the edges of the
borders. Glue confetti to
cards as shown in the
photograph, *above*. Let the
glue dry.

5 Use a silver marking
pen to draw ruled
borders on each card.

265

graphic greetings

Bold shapes and black eyelets team up for this funky Halloween note card. The varied paper edges are achieved using decorative-edge scissors.

supplies
Ruler
Pencil
Heavy paper in yellow, orange, black, and purple
Scissors, pinking shears, and desired decorative-edge scissors
Medium paper punch
Metal eyelets in white and black
Eyelet tool
Glue stick

what to do
1 Measure and cut a 3⅝×8¾-inch black rectangle using pinking shears. Cut a 3¼×8½-inch yellow rectangle. Cut a 3¼×1-inch strip from orange. Trim one long edge using pinking shears. Cut a 1⅛×1⅛-inch purple square using decorative-edge scissors. Cut a black triangle with 3-inch sides. Trim two of the sides with decorative-edge scissors.

2 On one short end of yellow paper, make six evenly spaced hole punches as shown in Photo 1, *right.* Place a black eyelet in each hole. Secure with eyelet tool as shown in Photo 2. Fold the yellow paper in half with the wrong side of the eyelets as the right side. Punch a hole in each corner of the black triangle. Secure a white eyelet in each hole. Again the wrong side of the eyelet will be used as the right side.

3 Glue the orange strip of paper behind the black eyelets, allowing the pinked edge of the orange paper to show beyond the edge of the yellow paper. Turn the purple square so it is a diamond shape and glue it in the center of the yellow card, 1 inch up from the short edge. Align the straight edge of the black triangle with the fold in the yellow paper. Glue the triangle to the card front.

1

2

4 Fold the black rectangle in half. Glue the yellow paper over black paper, aligning the folds. Let the glue dry.

bewitching invites

Create these clever invitations that use adhesive fingernails for a chilling effect.

supplies

Scissors; ruler
Black card stock
Scrapbook paper with white dots on black
Zigzag crafts scissors
Pencil; tracing paper
Green textured card stock

Paper punch
Black ribbon
Red adhesive fingernails
Strong glue, such as Beacon's Kids Choice

what to do

1 Cut an 11×3¼-inch rectangle from black card stock and scrapbook paper. Trim ½ inch from one short edge of the black

rectangle with zigzag crafts scissors.

2 Enlarge and trace the witch hand pattern, *left*. Cut out the pattern. Trace around the pattern on the green textured card stock and cut out the shape.

3 Lay the witch hand over the black rectangle and then lay them both over the dotted rectangle. Line up all the flat edges at the top. Punch two holes through all three layers. Thread a 7-inch-long ribbon through the holes and tie in a bow. Use glue to attach a fingernail to the forefinger. Let the glue dry.

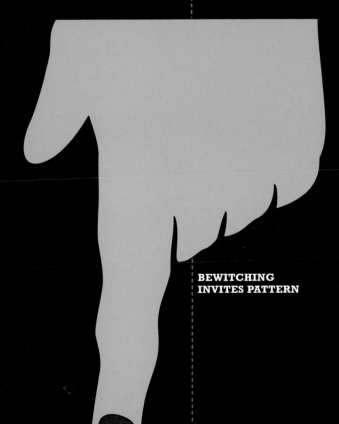

BEWITCHING INVITES PATTERN

269

beanbag toss

Ready...aim...toss! Kids love to play this party game, racking up points by tossing pumpkin-, ghost-, and cat-shape felt beanbags into the openings in the pumpkin. When not in use, place the pumpkin in the yard for all to see and enjoy.

supplies for pumpkin board
Pencil
4×4-foot ½-inch-thick exterior fir plywood
Jigsaw; sandpaper
Exterior paints in bright orange, dark orange, and black; paintbrush
1×4×30-inch fir board
1½×2½-inch butt hinge with screws
Screwdriver
16-inch light-duty chain with two ½-inch-long screws to fit
Drill and drill bit
24 inches of No. 9 wire

what to do
1 For the pumpkin board, enlarge the pumpkin pattern, *page 273,* and trace onto plywood. Cut out with

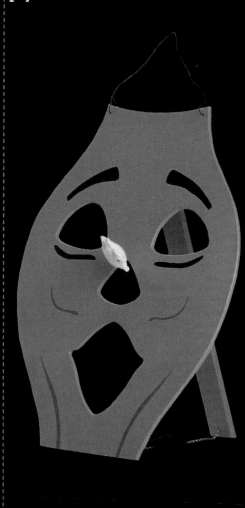

jigsaw. Cut out eyes, nose, and mouth. Sand the edges. Paint the entire pumpkin bright orange. Let dry. Paint the lines around the eyes black and the remaining lines dark orange.

2 Attach the fir board to back at top edge using hinge. Screw chain between brace and pumpkin at bottom edge. Drill holes in pumpkin 1½ inches from top and 4 inches from sides. Attach wire through the holes.

supplies for beanbags

(one of each shape)
Tracing paper
Pencil
Two 5-inch squares each of white and orange felt
Two 6-inch squares of black felt
Water-erasable marking pen
Scissors; ruler
Small scrap of green calico
Embroidery floss in black and white
Sewing needle
Thread; pin
Beans or rice
Pinking shears

what to do

1 For beanbags, enlarge the patterns, *page 272,* onto tracing paper. Transfer each design onto one square of felt (ghost on white, pumpkin on orange, and cat on black) using marking pen. (Note: Do not cut out.) Cut a 1½×2¾-inch rectangle from green calico for the pumpkin stem.

2 Using all six plies of the embroidery floss and referring to dots on patterns, work black French knots for ghost eyes, white French knots for cat eyes, and black Xs for pumpkin eyes. Work black backstitches for pumpkin smile.

3 For pumpkin stem, fold calico in half crosswise, right sides together, to form a ¾×1⅝-inch rectangle. Using ¼ inch seams, sew short sides. Turn right side out. Press under ¼ inch on raw edge.

4 For each shape, place the embroidered

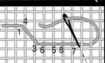

FRENCH KNOT (LEFT)

BACKSTITCH (BELOW)

square on an unstitched square, wrong sides facing. Pin pumpkin stem to top of pumpkin as indicated by Xs on pattern. Stitch along sewing line, leaving opening as indicated by slashes on pattern. Fill bags with beans or rice; sew openings closed. Cut out ¼ inch from seam using pinking shears.

continued on page 272

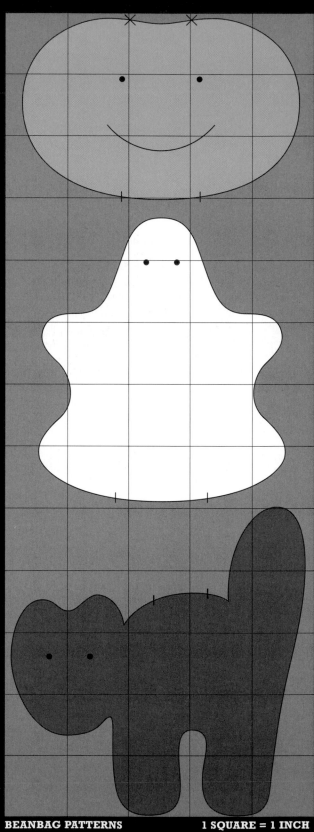

BEANBAG PATTERNS   1 SQUARE = 1 INCH

PUMPKIN BOARD PATTERN

1 SQUARE = 3 INCHES

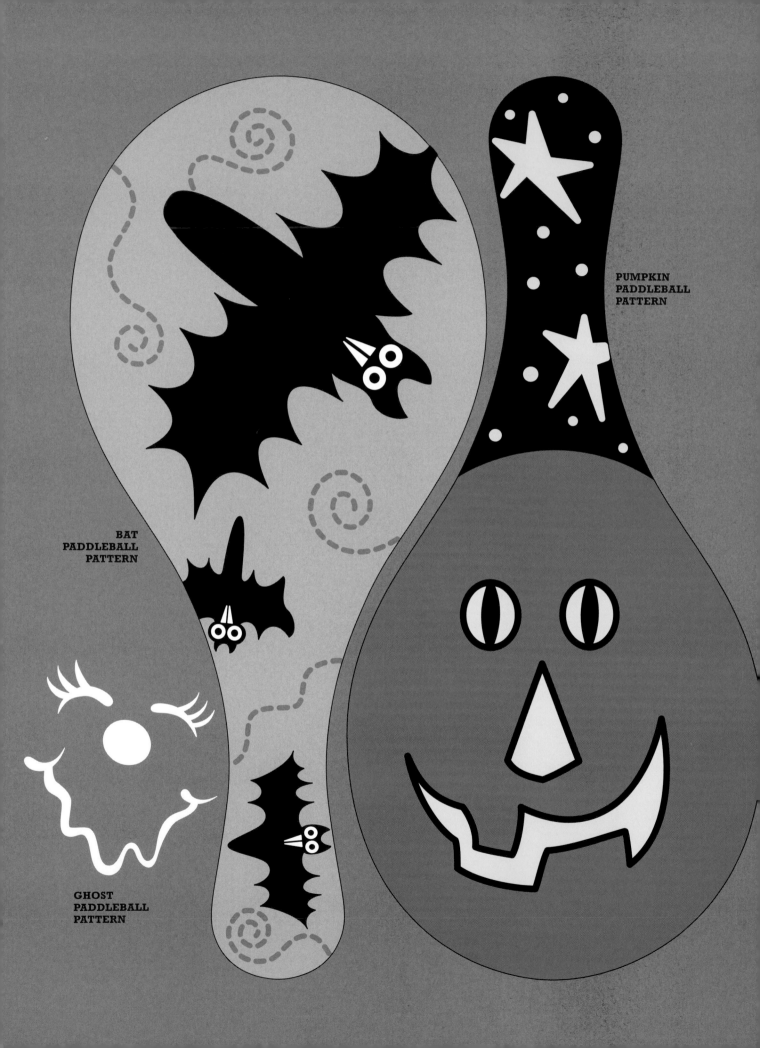

PUMPKIN
PADDLEBALL
PATTERN

BAT
PADDLEBALL
PATTERN

GHOST
PADDLEBALL
PATTERN

playful paddleballs

Young guests enjoy playing with (and taking home) these painted Halloween paddleball favors. Make them ahead using the patterns, opposite, or have the kids paint them at the party using their own Halloween designs. The paint dries quickly so the games are ready to go when the guests start heading for home.

supplies
Acrylic paints in black, white, gray, orange, and yellow
Paintbrush
Purchased paddleballs
Tracing paper
Pencil with round eraser
Transfer paper
Silver marking pen

what to do

1 Paint the background color of the design on the entire back and sides of the paddle. Paint the background for the ghost white, the pumpkin orange, and the bats gray. Let the paint dry.

2 Trace the desired patterns, *opposite.* Use transfer paper to transfer the details to the painted side of the paddleball. Paint in the details using the patterns as a guide. Let the paint dry. To make eyes on the bats, dip the eraser of a pencil or the handle of a paintbrush into white paint and dot onto the heads of the bats. Let the paint dry. Make smaller black dots in the center of each eye. Let the paint dry.

3 Use a silver marking pen to draw dotted-line swirls on the bat paddle.

4 Paint the attached balls using the photograph, *right,* for inspiration. Let the paint dry.

potion goblets

For a Halloween toast, raise these festive flutes filled with your favorite potion.

supplies
Clear glasses with long
  stems
Pipe cleaners in purple,
  orange, black, and
  lime green
Silver adhesive stars

what to do
1 Wash and dry the glasses. Beginning at the bottom of the stem, wrap tightly with a purple pipe cleaner. Continue wrapping the stem using the pipe cleaners as shown, *left.* When wrapping the top lime green pipe cleaner, wrap half of the length and then form the end into a spiral or zigzag shape.

2 Apply stars randomly to the outside of the glass top, avoiding the rim area. Remove the trims before washing the glass.

batty the lollipop holder

supplies
Tracing paper
Pencil
Scissors
Construction papers in black, orange, white, and lime green
Large- and medium-size paper punches
Glue stick
Fine-point marking pens in black and silver
Lollipop

what to do
1 Enlarge and trace the patterns and the hole positions, *below*. Cut out.

2 Trace around the bat shape on black paper, the banner on orange, and the fangs on white. Cut out the shapes. For the eyes, punch out two white circles using the large paper punch. Use the smaller punch to make a lime green nose. Glue the shapes into place.

3 Draw in the black and silver details and the lettering using marking pens. Fold the wings inward as shown in the photo, *above*. Punch two holes in each wing as shown. Align the hole punches; insert the lollipop stick through the holes.

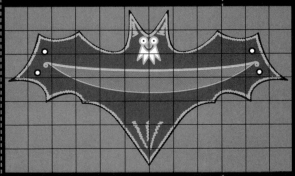

**BAT LOLLIPOP HOLDER
PATTERN—FRONT**　　　**1 SQUARE = 1 INCH**

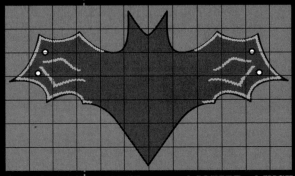

**BAT LOLLIPOP HOLDER
PATTERN—BACK**　　　**1 SQUARE = 1 INCH**

wizard hat ringtoss

Munchkins of all ages will love playing this game of skill at your next Halloween bash. The foam cone is glued on a terra-cotta base for weight. Wrapped with trims of all kinds, the cone makes good use of odds and ends. Once the plastic-lid rings are cut out, let the kids wrap them with pipe cleaners in their favorite Halloween colors.

supplies

2-inch foam ball, such as Styrofoam
Toothpick
Thick white crafts glue
12-inch-high foam cone, such as Styrofoam
6-inch terra-cotta flowerpot saucer
Hot-glue gun and glue sticks
Cording in silver, golden, purple, black, and green
Straight pins
Ribbon in purple, black, green, and orange
Scissors; ruler
Silver sequins on a string
1½-inch star sequins
Quilting pins
Plastic lids from large margarine containers
Pipe cleaners in orange, black, purple, silver, green, and golden

what to do

1 Press the foam ball against a hard, flat work surface to slightly flatten one side. Insert a toothpick halfway into the flattened side. Dab crafts glue on the flattened area of the ball and on the toothpick. Press into the top of the foam cone. Hot-glue the bottom of the cone to the bottom of the flowerpot saucer. Let dry.

2 Wrap the foam ball with silver cording, pinning the ends to secure. Wrap the saucer base with cording and ribbon using hot glue to adhere.

3 Cut 3-inch lengths from various widths of ribbon. Pin the ribbon pieces vertically at the bottom of the cone. Wrap the top of the cone using different colors of cording, ribbon, and silver sequin strings.

4 Cut a 24-inch length of silver cording. Wrap the cording diagonally around the cone, shaping the ends into spirals. Pin in place. Use quilting pins to secure star sequins by the cording spirals and randomly on the cone.

5 To make a ring, carefully cut the rim off a plastic lid. Cut a circle from the center of the lid, leaving a 1-inch ring. Wrap the ring with pipe cleaners.

6 To play, have players try to toss their rings onto the wizard hat.

mummy bowling

A new twist on an old favorite, this wide-eyed mummy bowling set will make youngsters howl.

supplies
Plastic bowling set
White spray primer, if needed
Black spray paint, if needed
Scissors

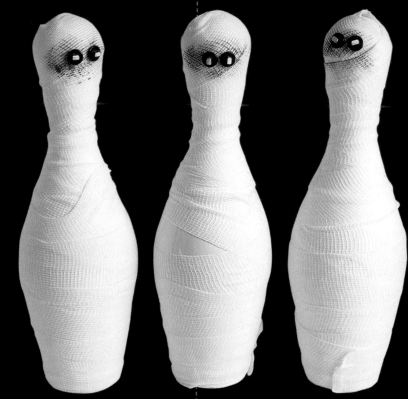

20 yards of 2- to 3-inch-wide gauze bandage; yardstick
Thick white crafts glue
Acrylic paints in green and orange
Paintbrush
¼-inch black buttons
Pencil with round eraser

what to do

1 If the bowling pins are colored, spray-paint them white in a well-ventilated work area. If the ball is not black, spray-paint it with primer. Let the paint dry. Spray-paint the ball black. Let dry.

2 Cut ten 2-yard lengths of gauze bandage. For each bowling pin, glue one end of the gauze at the bottom of the pin. Wrap the gauze to the top of the pin and back to the bottom, applying dabs of glue to secure. Let dry.

3 On the top of each pin, paint a green oval for the shading behind the eyes. Let the paint dry. For eyes, glue two black buttons side by side over the green painted area. Let dry.

4 To make dots on the bowling ball, dip the eraser of a pencil into orange paint and dot onto the surface. Let dry.

spider boxes

Use these printed spider boxes as fun dice shakers or to store small game pieces. To give them as a gift, tuck a piece or two of Halloween candy inside.

supplies
Rectangular plastic boxes with lids
Glass cleaner
Paper towels
Black acrylic paint
Disposable plate
Metallic pom-pom
Scrap paper
Black paint marking pen
Cotton swab; clear acrylic gloss sealer
Small wiggly eyes
Hot-glue gun and glue sticks
Small toys or candies

what to do
1 Remove labels and clean boxes with glass cleaner and paper towels.

2 Squeeze out a small amount of paint onto a disposable plate. For the spider body, dip the pom-pom into the paint and test print it onto scrap paper. When pleased with the results, print directly onto box and lid. Let the paint dry.

3 Use the paint pen to draw eight legs from the printed body. To make a foot, dip the cotton swab into the paint and test print it. Print a round foot at the end of each leg. Let the paint dry.

4 In a well-ventilated work area, spray a coat of sealer over the box. Let dry. Hot-glue two wiggly eyes onto the base of each printed body. Let the glue dry. Fill the box with small toys or candies.

jumpin' jack piñata

Made from a papier-mâché-covered balloon, this piñata holds a pumpkin full of treats inside its smile.

supplies
15-inch balloon
2 medium bowls
3 cups white flour
Water
Newspapers
Scissors
Tracing paper
Pencil
Medium-weight colored papers in black, purple, yellow, and orange
Crafts knife
Glue stick
Party hat in metallic blue or other color
Paper punch
Silver eyelets and eyelet tool
Lime green plastic lace
Yardstick
2 yards of ¼-inch-wide ribbon
Darning needle
Crepe paper streamers in orange and green
Small candies or plastic Halloween toys

what to do

1 Inflate the balloon and secure with a knot. Set the balloon in one of the bowls.

2 To make papier-mâché mixture, pour flour into a bowl. Stir in water until the mixture has the consistency of thick gravy.

3 Tear newspapers into strips. Dip one strip at a time in the flour mixture. Gently pull the strip between two fingers to remove excess. Place wet strip on balloon as shown in Photo 1, *right.* Cover the balloon with two to three layers of paper strips, leaving only the balloon knot exposed. Turn the balloon over in the bowl and repeat. Let dry. Remove balloon from bowl. Holding the balloon by the knot, puncture the balloon and remove from the hardened piñata.

4 Enlarge and trace the patterns, *pages 284–285.* Cut out patterns. Trace around patterns on colored papers. Cut out shapes. Trace around one eye pattern on small end of piñata in eye area. Use a crafts knife to cut out

eye shape, ¼ inch inside the drawn line.

5 Glue the black pieces for the yellow eyes and the purple stripes for the hands and legs. Cut a 10-inch circle from black paper for the hat brim. Place the party hat in the center of the paper circle. Trace the party hat. Cut out slightly inside the circle. Glue the party hat to the brim. Let dry.

6 Using the pattern as a guide, punch holes along the tops of both shoes. Use an eyelet tool to secure eyelets in each hole as shown, *opposite.* Cut two 24-inch lengths of lime green plastic lace. Lace through eyelets and tie ends into a bow. Glue shoes to legs. Let the glue dry.

7 Use a crafts knife to cut two small holes in the top of the piñata. Insert ribbon into needle. Sew through holes in piñata top. Remove the needle. Knot the ribbon ends to secure.

8 Cut 4 yards of crepe paper streamers at a time. Wrap paper into a 1-foot loop. Carefully cut ½-inch-wide fringes

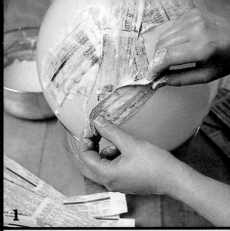

1

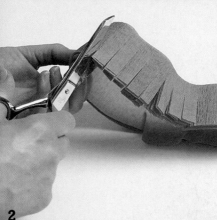

2

3

along one side of the loop, being careful not to trim through the edges, as shown in Photo 2, *above.*

continued on page 284

9 Beginning at the bottom (large end) of the piñata, wind and glue unfringed edge of crepe paper streamers onto the piñata, as shown in Photo 3, *page 283.* Continue wrapping and gluing until the piñata is covered. Through the eye opening, fill the piñata with candies or toys.

10 Pleat the arms. Glue the paper pieces onto the piñata, covering cutout eye area with a paper eye. Let dry.

11 Tie a bow from green crepe paper. Glue onto hat. Let dry.

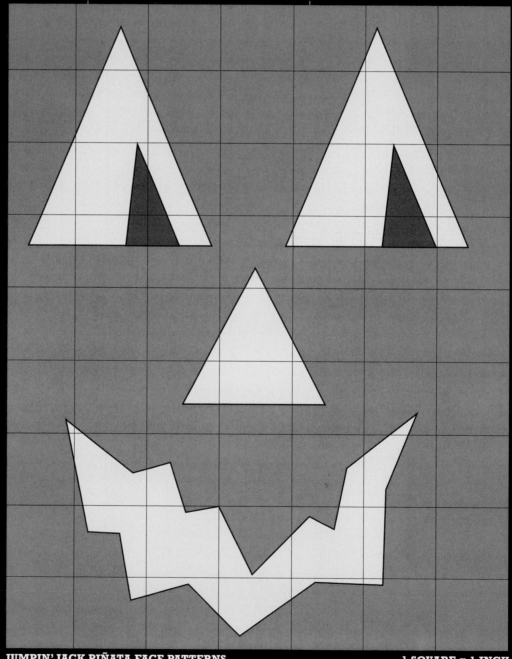

JUMPIN' JACK PIÑATA FACE PATTERNS   1 SQUARE = 1 INCH

JUMPIN' JACK PIÑATA ARM AND LEG PATTERNS

1 SQUARE = 1 INCH

continued on page 288

index continued

DESIGNERS
Susan Banker, Donna
Chesnut, Carol Dahlstrom,
Alice Wetzel
PHOTOSTYLING
Carol Dahlstrom, Donna
Chesnut, assistant
PHOTOGRAPHY
Andy Lyons Cameraworks,
Peter Krumhardt, Scott Little